Lewis Howard Latimer

an E. Matzeliger

George Washington Carver

Madam C. J. Walker

Garrett A. Morgan

Percy Lavon Julian

Patricia Era Bath

Lonnie G. Johnson

Inspiring
African-American
Inventors

9 **Extraordinary Lives**

Granville T. Woods
Most Inspiring Invention:
Developed the System That Allowed Train
Engineers to Talk to Train Stations,
Making Rail Travel Safer.

Jeff C. Young

MyReportLinks.com Books

Enslow Publishers, Inc.
Box 398, 40 Industrial Road
Berkeley Heights, NJ 07922
USA

To my good friend, William D. Penmann, D.D.

MyReportLinks.com Books, an imprint of Enslow Publishers, Inc. MyReportLinks®
is a registered trademark of Enslow Publishers, Inc.

Library of Congress Cataloging-in-Publication Data

Young, Jeff C., 1948–
  Inspiring African-American inventors: nine extraordinary lives / Jeff C. Young.
      p. cm. — (Great scientists and famous inventors)
  Includes bibliographical references and index.
  ISBN-13: 978-1-59845-080-4 (hardcover : alk. paper)
  ISBN-10: 1-59845-080-8 (hardcover : alk. paper)
  1. African American inventors—Biography—Juvenile literature. I. Title.
T39.Y685 2008
608.996'073—dc22
[B]
                                2007022937

Printed in the United States of America

10 9 8 7 6 5 4 3 2 1

To Our Readers:
Through the purchase of this book, you and your library gain access to the Report Links that specifically back up this book.
The Publisher will provide access to the Report Links that back up this book and will keep these Report Links up to date on **www.myreportlinks.com** for five years from the book's first publication date.
We have done our best to make sure all Internet addresses in this book were active and appropriate when we went to press. However, the author and the Publisher have no control over, and assume no liability for, the material available on those Internet sites or on other Web sites they may link to.
The usage of the MyReportLinks.com Books Web site is subject to the terms and conditions stated on the Usage Policy Statement on **www.myreportlinks.com**.
A password may be required to access the Report Links that back up this book. The password is found on the bottom of page 4 of this book.
Any comments or suggestions can be sent by e-mail to comments@myreportlinks.com or to the address on the back cover.

♻ Enslow Publishers, Inc., is committed to printing our books on recycled paper. The paper in every book contains 10% to 30% post-consumer waste (PCW). The cover board on the outside of each book contains 100% PCW. Our goal is to do our part to help young people and the environment too!

Photo Credits: About.com, a part of The New York Times Company, p. 6; AfricanAmericans.com, p. 106; A'Lelia Bundles, p. 66; American Heritage Publishing, p. 24; AP/Wide World Photos, pp. 86, 92, 114; Chemical Heritage Foundation, p. 90; Courtesy Patricia E. Bath, M.D., pp. 98, 104; DePauw University, p. 96; Famous Black Inventors, p. 57; General Electric, p. 12; Indiana Historical Society, p. 73; Inventors Assistance League, p. 42; John H. Lienhard, pp. 31, 78; Johnson Research & Development, pp. 108, 112, 116; Library of Congress, pp. 46, 53, 54–55, 58–59, 62–63, 71; Madam C. J. Walker Collection, Courtesy of the Indiana Historical Society, pp. 60, 68–69; Massachusetts Institute of Technology, pp. 29, 100, 117; National Inventors Hall of Fame Foundation, p. 44; National Park Service, pp. 16, 48; NESTA, p. 36; NMSI, p. 77; NYPA, p. 18; President and Fellows of Harvard College, p. 64; Queens Borough Library, Long Island Division, Latimer Family Papers, pp. 10, 15; Shutterstock.com, pp. 32, 40–41, 94; Smithsonian Institution, pp. 20, 103; Southern California Edison, p. 7; The Field Museum, p. 51; The Granger Collection, New York, pp. 22, 27, 34; The New York Times, p. 110; The Ohio Historical Society, p. 38; The Western Reserve Historical Society, Cleveland, Ohio, pp. 74, 80–81; U.S. Department of Commerce, p. 9; U.S. Patent and Trademark Office, p. 83; WGBH, pp. 84, 88.

Cover Photo: The Granger Collection, New York

CONTENTS

About MyReportLinks.com Books 4

Introduction 5

1 ▶ LEWIS HOWARD LATIMER 10

2 ▶ JAN E. MATZELIGER 22

3 ▶ GRANVILLE T. WOODS 34

4 ▶ GEORGE WASHINGTON CARVER 46

5 ▶ MADAM C. J. WALKER 60

6 ▶ GARRETT A. MORGAN 74

7 ▶ PERCY LAVON JULIAN 86

8 ▶ PATRICIA ERA BATH 98

9 ▶ LONNIE G. JOHNSON 108

Report Links 118

Glossary 120

Chapter Notes 122

Further Reading 125

Index 126

MyReportLinks.com Books
Great Books, Great Links, Great for Research!

The Internet sites featured in this book can save you hours of research time. These Internet sites—we call them **"Report Links"**—are constantly changing, but we keep them up to date on our Web site.

When you see this "Approved Web Site" logo, you will know that we are directing you to a great Internet site that will help you with your research.

Give it a try! Type http://www.myreportlinks.com into your browser, click on the series title and enter the password, then click on the book title, and scroll down to the Report Links listed for this book.

The Report Links will bring you to great source documents, photographs, and illustrations. MyReportLinks.com Books save you time, feature Report Links that are kept up to date, and make report writing easier than ever! A complete listing of the Report Links can be found on pages 118–119 at the back of the book.

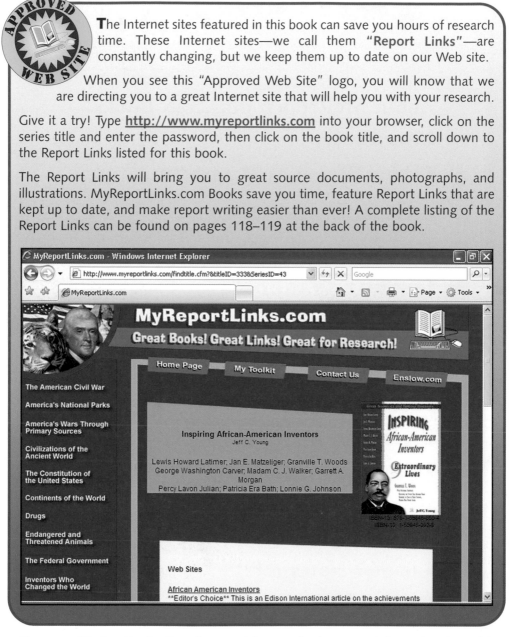

Please see "To Our Readers" on the copyright page for important information about this book, the MyReportLinks.com Web site, and the Report Links that back up this book.

Please enter **IAA1862** if asked for a password.

Introduction

*I*t is a sad fact that America was not always supportive of African-American inventors. Before America abolished slavery in 1865, only free African Americans were allowed to patent an invention. Even then, the process of securing all rights to the creation was difficult. Because of racial attitudes, African Americans were not widely perceived as having the intelligence and ingenuity to become inventors. Still, both slaves and free African Americans were able to use their technical knowledge and skills to invent new devices and techniques in such fields as agriculture, boat building, and making musical instruments. Only many never received the lawful credit due them.

After the enactment of the United States Patent Act in 1790, there was some record of the works of African-American inventors. But that documentation is sketchy because the U.S. Patent Office usually did not record or ask for the race of the inventor. The act, which granted individuals patents (of up to fourteen years at a time) for inventions considered valuable and practical, only required a

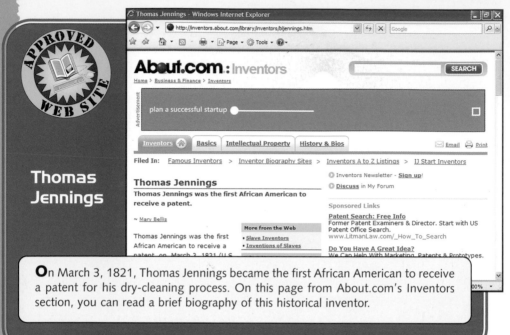

Thomas Jennings

On March 3, 1821, Thomas Jennings became the first African American to receive a patent for his dry-cleaning process. On this page from About.com's Inventors section, you can read a brief biography of this historical inventor.

Access this Web site from http://www.myreportlinks.com

clear and detailed description of the device being submitted. Thomas L. Jennings was the first African-American inventor to receive a patent. In 1821, he received a patent for a dry-cleaning process that he invented.

Even after slavery was abolished, there were other obstacles faced by African-American inventors. They did not have the same access to apprenticeships, training, and education as whites. It was not until 1833 that Oberlin University in Ohio became the first American university to admit African Americans. Many states, particularly in the South, enforced policies that created "separate but equal" status for blacks, but in reality led to treatment inferior to whites. Those policies often prevented African Americans from nurturing their inventive skills and interacting with other inventors.

Between 1857 and 1871 several predominantly African-American colleges and universities were founded, but their curriculums offered few classes in the sciences and technology. Their major focus was on preparing African Americans to become teachers, doctors, nurses, or clergymen.

African-American inventors also found it difficult to find investors to finance their research and help

On the **African American Inventors** Web site, you will find biographies of a number of African Americans who have made important contributions to society. Among those included are Patricia Bath, Andrew Beard, and Michael Croslin.

EDITOR'S CHOICE

market their inventions after they were patented. Sometimes, the inventor would have to give up the rights to his or her work to get the financial backing needed. The inventor's name might appear on the patent, but he or she would not make any money from the sales of the invention.

In the 1900s there was a large migration of African Americans from the rural South to the northern cities. The growth of industries in transportation and other manufacturing fields led to the establishment of many factories needing large numbers of workers. About 2 million African Americans left the southern countryside for work opportunities in the quickly growing cities of the North.[1]

African Americans that used to work on farms developed technical skills from working in factories and machine shops. Exposure to new technologies brought out their inventive nature. They looked for new ways of doing things and improving the quality of life for other Americans. Their accomplishments belied the belief that African Americans lacked the intellectual capacity to become inventors.

Changes in technology spurred some of the inventors profiled in this book to create. When electricity became a major energy source, inventors Granville Woods and Lewis Latimer found new uses for that emerging technology. When

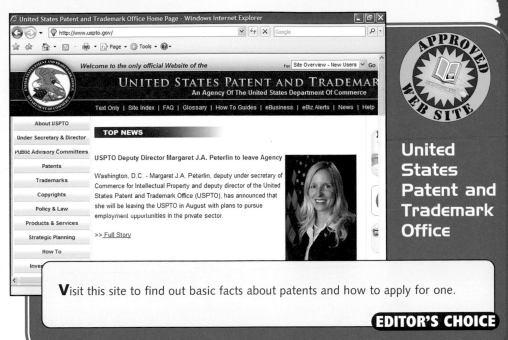

United States Patent and Trademark Office Home Page - Windows Internet Explorer

http://www.uspto.gov/

Welcome to the only official Website of the

UNITED STATES PATENT AND TRADEMAR

An Agency Of The United States Department Of Commerce

Text Only | Site Index | FAQ | Glossary | How To Guides | eBusiness | eBiz Alerts | News | Help

About USPTO
Under Secretary & Director
Public Advisory Committees
Patents
Trademarks
Copyrights
Policy & Law
Products & Services
Strategic Planning
How To
Inve

TOP NEWS

USPTO Deputy Director Margaret J.A. Peterlin to leave Agency

Washington, D.C. - Margaret J.A. Peterlin, deputy under secretary of Commerce for Intellectual Property and deputy director of the United States Patent and Trademark Office (USPTO), has announced that she will be leaving the USPTO in August with plans to pursue employment opportunities in the private sector.

>> Full Story

APPROVED WEB SITE

United States Patent and Trademark Office

Visit this site to find out basic facts about patents and how to apply for one.

EDITOR'S CHOICE

Access this Web site from http://www.myreportlinks.com

automobiles became commonplace, Garrett A. Morgan found a way to make the roads safer.

Other inventors like Percy Julian looked for ways to ease human pain and suffering. His pioneering work in using the soybean to synthesize drugs made medicines more abundant and affordable for people all over the world.

Besides their race, one thing that all nine of these inventors had in common was an enduring belief in themselves and a determination to succeed. In some way, all of them made the world they lived in a better place.

Lewis Howard Latimer

lexander Graham Bell and Thomas Alva Edison are well known and remembered as two great American inventors. Bell invented the telephone and Edison is famous for inventing the electric lightbulb and the phonograph. One thing not well known, though, is the

Lifeline

1864: Enlists in U.S. Navy during The Civil War.

1880: Moves to New York City.

1848: Born in Chelsea, Massachusetts, on September 4.

1874: Awarded first patent for improving a railroad car toilet.

invaluable help they received from Lewis H. Latimer.

Unlike most African Americans of his time, Latimer was born a free man. His parents were runaway slaves who escaped from Virginia and settled in Boston. His father, George, was later arrested in Boston for being a runaway slave, but he was set free after three famous abolitionist leaders—William Lloyd Garrison, Frederick Douglass, and the Reverend Samuel Caldwell—paid four hundred dollars for his freedom.

Latimer was born in Chelsea, an outer suburb of Boston, Massachusetts, on September 4, 1848. He had two older brothers and one sister. His family never had much money and Latimer had to neglect his education often to work and earn money. During the brief time he attended school, he was a very good

Chapter 1

1886: Awarded patent for a type of room air conditioner.

1928: Died in Flushing (Queens), New York, on December 11.

1882: Patents a carbon filament for use in electric lightbulbs.

1896: Publishes book, Incandescent Electric Lighting.

student. He enjoyed art, reading, and creative writing, and he was allowed to skip a grade.

When he was only ten, Latimer had to quit school. For some reason, his father left or became separated from his family. Some writers and historians believe that George was afraid of being recaptured by slave catchers.[1] With the family's primary source of income gone, Lewis Latimer had no choice but to begin working full time. He did odd jobs as well as working as a waiter.

In 1864, Latimer lied about his age and enlisted in the U.S. Navy during the Civil War. He

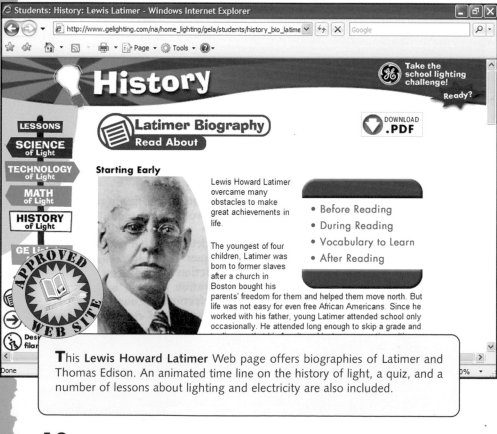

This **Lewis Howard Latimer** Web page offers biographies of Latimer and Thomas Edison. An animated time line on the history of light, a quiz, and a number of lessons about lighting and electricity are also included.

served as a cabin boy on the USS *Massasoit* until the war ended in 1865.

⚗ PERSISTENCE BRINGS PATENT

After his honorable discharge from the Navy, Latimer returned to Boston. In 1871 he went to work for Crosby, Halsted, & Gould, a firm of patent lawyers, at a weekly salary of three dollars. His job there as an office boy allowed him to watch the firm's draftsmen draw models of inventions.

Latimer became fascinated with their work. He bought a book on drawing and some used drawing tools. He began to spend his evenings working on drawings. His persistence paid off when he was promoted from office boy to junior draftsman.

Eventually, Latimer became the firm's top draftsman. Along with drawings of inventions, he learned how to make working models of inventions. Latimer also learned how inventions were patented. With a few of his own original ideas brewing inside, Latimer decided to take a stab at becoming an inventor himself.

In 1874, Latimer was awarded his first patent. He and Charles W. Brown patented a pivot bottom for toilets on railroad cars. When the toilet lid was raised, the pivoted bottom automatically closed. That prevented debris and wind from coming in from the outdoors. When the lid was

13

closed, the pivot bottom automatically opened so the toilet would flush.

Shortly after receiving his first patent, Latimer met Alexander Graham Bell, who taught at a school for the deaf in Boston. Bell asked Latimer to draw the schematic plans for a machine that would become known as the telephone. He also had Latimer assist with writing the descriptions of his invention for the patent application. That machine was patented in 1876 as the first telephone.

🧪 MORE OPPORTUNITIES

In 1880, Latimer moved to New York City. Inventor Hiram S. Maxim, the chief electrician and founder of United States Electric Lighting Company, quickly went knocking on Latimer's door. Latimer was hired to be the Connecticut-based company's assistant manager and draftsman. Maxim's company was competing with Edison's company for a share of the emerging electrical lighting market.

Latimer began studying and learning all about electrical lights and lighting. That led to Latimer's most important invention. In 1882, Latimer patented a carbon filament for electrical lightbulbs. The new filament increased both the brightness and life of electric bulbs. Its use made

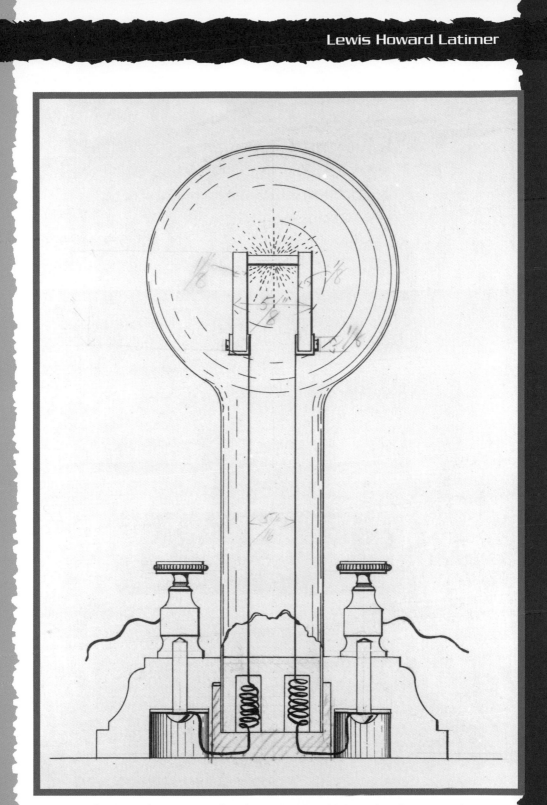

▲ On the back of this drawing, Latimer noted, "The first drawing made by me for Hiram Maxim was made from drawing in Bridgeport, Conn in 1880."

electrical lighting more commonplace and affordable.

During his employment with Maxim, Latimer did a lot of traveling. He oversaw the establishment of factories and the installation of lighting systems in Philadelphia, New York City, London, and Montreal. During his time in Montreal, he taught himself French.

Latimer also continued to patent other inventions to improve the quality and dependability of electrical lighting. He patented two inventions for an electric lamp and a globe-shaped base for electrical lamps.

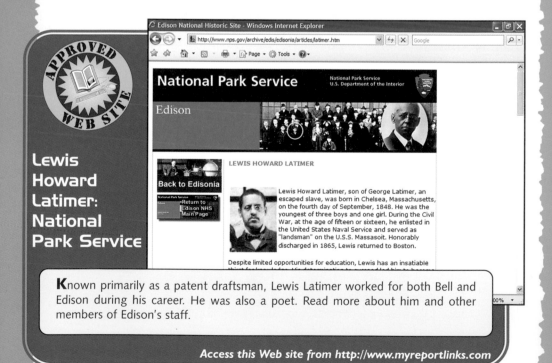

Lewis
Howard
Latimer:
National
Park Service

Known primarily as a patent draftsman, Lewis Latimer worked for both Bell and Edison during his career. He was also a poet. Read more about him and other members of Edison's staff.

Access this Web site from http://www.myreportlinks.com

WORKING WITH EDISON

In 1883, Latimer left Maxim's company. He briefly worked for the Olmstead Electrical Lighting Company in Brooklyn, New York, before being hired by the Edison Electric Light Company across the river in New Jersey. Thomas Alva Edison was one of America's most prolific inventors. He was granted patents for more than one thousand inventions. But while he was a great inventor, he was often a poor businessman and record keeper.

Edison usually spent money faster than it came in. Many times, he had to revise his patent applications because he left out important details. Latimer was detail oriented and had a thorough knowledge of the patent process. During his long tenure with Edison's company, Latimer became a very valuable employee.

Along with his expertise in the patenting process, Latimer was well versed in electrical lighting and electrical power systems. Other inventors would infringe on Edison's patents by using his work without his permission. Many of Edison's patent infringement lawsuits involved European inventors and businesses. Latimer was able to translate articles from German and French into English. That helped Edison's company learn about unauthorized use of Edison's inventions.

▲ Furniture of the era, as well as informational displays about Lewis Latimer can be viewed at his home in Queens, New York City.

🧪 OTHER CREATIONS

While working for Edison, Latimer was still able to pursue other inventions of his own. In 1886 he was granted a patent for an early version of the room air conditioner. Latimer's invention had a wet cloth stretched over a wooden frame. At the top of the cloth there was a reservoir for holding chemicals to purify the air. At the bottom, there was a drip pan to collect any spillover.

His invention both cooled and purified the air in the room. In his patent application, Latimer wrote: "The object of my invention is to present a large evaporating surface for the purpose of cooling the air about or passing over it, or to charge the same with chemical agents . . . to destroy such odors or germs of disease that may exist."[2]

Along with his inventing, Latimer was a prolific writer. His 1896 book, *Incandescent Electric Lighting*, was one of the first textbooks on the subject. A book of his poems was published by his friends on Latimer's seventy-fifth birthday. He also wrote a play.

In 1896, General Electric and Westinghouse created the Board of Patent Control to monitor patent disputes and prosecute patent infringers. Latimer became the board's chief draftsman and was an expert witness in lawsuits. After the board was disbanded in 1911, he worked as a patent law

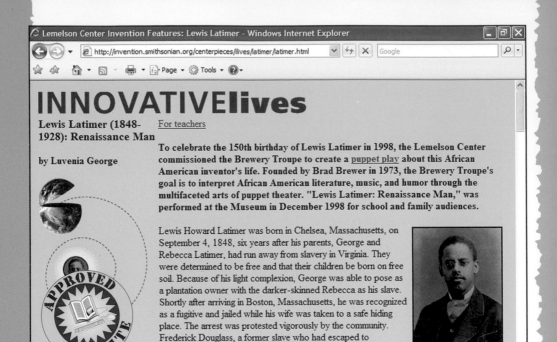

Lemelson Center Invention Features: Lewis Latimer - Windows Internet Explorer

http://invention.smithsonian.org/centerpieces/ilives/latimer/latimer.html

Google

Page ▾ Tools ▾

INNOVATIVElives

Lewis Latimer (1848-1928): Renaissance Man

For teachers

by Luvenia George

To celebrate the 150th birthday of Lewis Latimer in 1998, the Lemelson Center commissioned the Brewery Troupe to create a puppet play about this African American inventor's life. Founded by Brad Brewer in 1973, the Brewery Troupe's goal is to interpret African American literature, music, and humor through the multifaceted arts of puppet theater. "Lewis Latimer: Renaissance Man," was performed at the Museum in December 1998 for school and family audiences.

Lewis Howard Latimer was born in Chelsea, Massachusetts, on September 4, 1848, six years after his parents, George and Rebecca Latimer, had run away from slavery in Virginia. They were determined to be free and that their children be born on free soil. Because of his light complexion, George was able to pose as a plantation owner with the darker-skinned Rebecca as his slave. Shortly after arriving in Boston, Massachusetts, he was recognized as a fugitive and jailed while his wife was taken to a safe hiding place. The arrest was protested vigorously by the community. Frederick Douglass, a former slave who had escaped to Massachusetts several years earlier, and abolitionist William Lloyd

Lewis Latimer was an African-American draftsman and inventor. He worked for Edison as a patent investigator and expert witness in patent litigation. Find out more about his life and inventions at the **Lewis Latimer (1848–1928): Renaissance Man** Web page.

consultant for the New York City firm of Hammer & Schwartz.

A HELPING, CARING PERSON

Outside of his work, Latimer involved himself in civil-rights issues and New York City politics. He taught evening classes in English and mechanical drawing to immigrants from Eastern Europe. Latimer also found time to work with younger inventors and guide them through the patent application process.

A stroke in 1924 forced Latimer to retire from his consulting work. He spent the last four years of his life in New York drawing, sketching, and writing poetry. Latimer died on December 11, 1928. Along with his writing and inventions, Latimer is remembered for being a helpful person dedicated to improving people's lives.

Latimer's granddaughter, Winifred Latimer Norman, summed up his very productive life by saying, "My grandfather had a feeling of mission, I believe. . . . which came originally from his father and also his philosophy of life. It had to do with the brotherhood of man."[3]

Jan E. Matzeliger

Shoes are something so commonplace most people do not realize that they were not always readily available. Today, you can go into any shoe store and find dozens of styles, sizes, and colors that are comfortable,

Lifeline

1877: *Moves to Lynn, Massachusetts.*

1852: *Born in Paramaribo, Suriname, on September 15.*

1882: *Finishes scrap model of a shoe-lasting machine.*

affordable, and attractive. Thanks to an inventor named Jan Matzeliger, it is easy to find shoes that are just right for you.

Matzeliger was born in the South American country of Dutch Guiana on September 15, 1852. Today, Dutch Guiana is known as Suriname. His father was a Dutch engineer and his Surinamese mother may have been born in West Africa. Matzeliger's father was in charge of the government's machine shops. Jan began working as an apprentice in one of those shops when he was only ten.

As an apprentice, Jan Matzeliger showed a natural talent for working with machines and mechanical devices. When he was in his teens, he had learned enough to become a skilled machinist. But he was restless and he wanted to leave Suriname. When he was

1883: Receives patent for shoe-lasting machine.

1889: Died in Lynn, Massachusetts, on August 24.

1885: His machine is able to last 75 pairs of women's shoes in a day.

1901: Awarded gold medal and diploma from Pan-American Exposition.

AmericanHeritage.com / AGAINST ALL ODDS - Windows Internet Explorer

http://www.americanheritage.com/articles/magazine/it/1991/3/1991_3_50.sh

AmericanHeritage.com
History's Homepage

Login | Register
Make this your homepage

Home | People | Places | Events | Entertainment | Magazine | **Invention & Technology** | Travel | Blog | Discussions

Search | Search Our Invention & Technology Article Archives | Invention & Technology ▾ | Search

Most Popular Searches: Thomas Paine | Thomas Jefferson | Music | Great Depression | Edison

Invention & Technology Magazine

Winter 1991   Volume 6, Issue 3

Against All Odds

Browse Archives

Browse our *Invention & Technology* Magazine issues from 1985 to the present.

Archives >>

Special Features

Subscriber Services: American Heritage

Subscriber

Vibram shoe
1,000+ Shoes. Huge Selection. Find vibram shoes

Foot Care Insoles
Professional Footcare Products Get PROFOOT money saving coupons
Ads by Google

AGAINST ALL ODDS

Jan Matzeliger, a poor black immigrant, struggled alone to become an inventor and in the early 1880s succeeded in devising a machine that revolutionized the industry

by Dennis Karwatka

If most nineteenth-century American inventors are forgotten today—which is

HIDDEN MYSTERIES CIVIL WAR

Play it

Learn about Jan Matzeliger's rise from a poor African-American immigrant to inventor of a machine that revolutionized the shoe industry.

Access this Web site from http://www.myreportlinks.com

nineteen, he began working as a merchant seaman for the Dutch East Indies Company.

FROM STEAMSHIPS TO SHOES

For the next two years, Matzeliger was able to visit many ports while learning how to maintain and repair steamship engines. He decided that Philadelphia, Pennsylvania, was the port where he would settle down. Matzeliger started looking for work as a machinist. In spite of his knowledge and skills, he had trouble finding work in his chosen field.

Unfortunately, racial discrimination kept African Americans from working as machinists.

In addition, Matzeliger was hindered by his lack of communication skills. He spoke little English. In Suriname, Dutch had been the national language. Eventually, he found work in a shoemaker's shop.

While working there, Matzeliger learned to use a machine that sewed the soles onto shoes. He also learned how to operate the other machines in the shop. Matzeliger became immersed in the shoe-making process and thought about ways to increase production.

When he was not working as a shoemaker or thinking about the industry, Matzeliger worked to improve his language skills. He went to night school and learned how to speak English without an accent. He read a lot and studied physics and other subjects. Matzeliger also painted pictures and supplemented his income by giving art lessons.

IMPROVING THE "LAST" STEP

In 1877, Jan Matzeliger moved to Lynn, Massachusetts, the shoe manufacturing center of North America. He made the rounds of several factories before getting hired by the Harney Brothers shoe factory.

Matzeliger noticed that every step of the shoe-making process was automated—except for the final step, which was called lasting. Lasting is the job of connecting the upper part of the shoe to the sole. Lasting is responsible for how well the shoe fits and looks. The workers who did the job of lasting knew how important their work was. Oftentimes, they could not keep up with the quantity of shoe pieces being produced by machines. Usually, there was a backlog of shoe pieces waiting for them. Having a strong union to protect them, the lasters would work slowly and often go on strike. They were called the kings of the shoe-making trade.

Matzeliger requested, and got, a job as a millwright at the Harney Brothers factory. That allowed him to check on and repair all of the shoe-making machines. It also gave him the chance to watch the lasters at work and learn exactly what they did.

Jan Matzeliger rented a room and converted it into a lab for working on a shoe-lasting machine. He did not tell anyone about his work because he knew that other inventors had the same idea. After about six months, Matzeliger had assembled a model of his machine. It was made from old cigar boxes, scrap wood, nails, and wire. When another inventor offered Jan fifty dollars for his crude model, Matzeliger wisely turned him down. Although the offer was not a very large amount, that the machine sparked interest told Matzeliger that he was on the right track.

Now he was ready to build a sturdier, more durable model. Matzeliger salvaged parts from

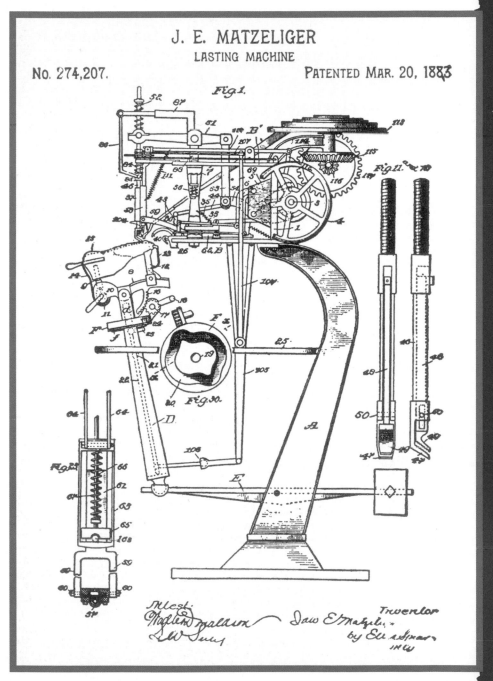

junkyards, old castings, and broken-down machines. Still, he was lacking the machines he needed to perfect and complete his invention. He needed a forge (furnace) for heating metal and a lathe (a machine that rotates an object) for shaping the metal parts. He left Harney Brothers and began working for Beal Brothers to get access to the needed machines.

Matzeliger's new employer was supportive of his efforts. Along with access to the machines, the company gave him a workspace to pursue his invention. Even though the lathe and forge were old machines and not easy to use, Matzeliger did not let that discourage him. He had come too far to give up.

While working on his machine, Matzeliger lived on just a few cents a day. Most of his income went to completing his invention. He took on a second job driving a coach that transported children to a local park.

Sometime in 1882, Matzeliger finished the scrap metal model of his shoe-lasting machine. This time another inventor offered him fifteen hundred dollars for the model. Matzeliger badly needed the money, but he turned the offer down. He never quit believing in himself and his idea. His second model worked, but it did not stand up to factory testing. He would have to build yet another model with new, rather than used parts.

At MIT's **Inventor of the Week: Jan Matzeliger**, you will find a short biography of this famous inventor.

🧪 *WILL IT LAST?*

Matzeliger began looking for financial backers for his shoe-lasting machine venture. He was repeatedly turned down before two businessmen agreed to finance his invention. In return, Matzeliger agreed to give them two-thirds of the profits from his machine. His two backers, Charles H. Denlow and Melville S. Nichols, founded the Union Lasting Machine Company. Matzeliger began working on his third model and applied for a patent.

29

When the Patent Office officials in Washington, D.C., received Matzeliger's detailed plans they could not understand his complicated drawings. The doubtful officials also did not believe that his machine could do what he claimed. They sent an examiner to the city of Lynn to inspect the invention.

Matzeliger demonstrated his machine to the examiner. He showed him that it could do everything that he claimed. The examiner was satisfied. On March 20, 1883, Matzeliger received U.S. Patent No. 274,207 for his shoe-lasting machine.

The machine still had to pass a test under factory conditions. On May 29, 1885, his amazing machine lasted seventy-five pairs of women's shoes with no problems. Later on, it was able to last one hundred fifty to seven hundred pairs of shoes in one day.

THE WAITING PAYS OFF

By the mid-1880s, every shoe manufacturer in Lynn was buying and using Matzeliger's shoe-lasting machine. Shoe manufacturing became a booming business and shoe prices were cut in half. The machine had revolutionized the industry. Instead of putting shoe lasters out of work, Matzeliger's invention made their jobs easier and increased their productivity. Their daily output was increased by up to 1,000 percent.

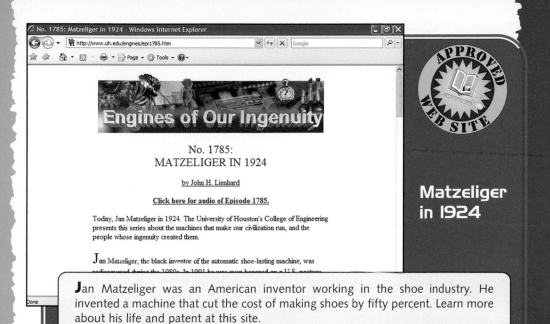

No. 1785: Matzeliger in 1924 - Windows Internet Explorer

http://www.uh.edu/engines/epi1785.htm

Google

Page · Tools ·

Engines of Our Ingenuity

No. 1785:
MATZELIGER IN 1924

by John H. Lienhard

Click here for audio of Episode 1785.

Today, Jan Matzeliger in 1924. The University of Houston's College of Engineering presents this series about the machines that make our civilization run, and the people whose ingenuity created them.

Jan Matzeliger, the black inventor of the automatic shoe-lasting machine, was

Matzeliger in 1924

Jan Matzeliger was an American inventor working in the shoe industry. He invented a machine that cut the cost of making shoes by fifty percent. Learn more about his life and patent at this site.

Access this Web site from http://www.myreportlinks.com

Jan Matzeliger continued to work on modifying and improving his invention until he died of tuberculosis on August 24, 1889. He received four additional patents for various improvements to the machine. At the time of his death—one month shy of his thirty-seventh birthday—there was a worldwide demand for Matzeliger's shoe-lasting machine.

In spite of his great success, Jan did not make any big changes in the way he lived. He continued to teach oil painting classes and he taught Sunday school. He was remembered for being a polite, cheerful, and friendly man. He supported his church after his death by willing all of his holdings

▲ Before the invention of Matzeliger's shoe-lasting machine, cobblers would spend many hours attaching soles to shoes by hand.

in the Union Lasting Machine Company (by this time, known the Consolidated Lasting Machine Company) to it.

Like some other inventors, Jan Matzeliger received greater recognition for his work after his death. In 1901 the Pan-American Exposition awarded him their Gold Medal and Diploma.

Granville T. Woods

Granville T. Woods was such a prolific inventor he became known as the Black Edison. Like Edison, Woods had a fascination and a deep curiosity about machines and electricity. Also, like Edison, he left school at an early age and was largely self-educated. Unlike Edison, Woods's many inventions never made him much money. Woods died in poverty.

Lifeline

1884: Receives first patent for steam-boiler furnace.

1887: Receives patent for "Synchronous Multiplex Railway Telegraph."

1856: Born in Columbus, Ohio, on April 23.

1885: Patents his "Telegraphony" system of communication.

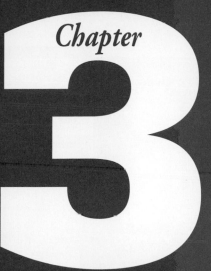

Woods was born in Columbus, Ohio, on April 23, 1856. Little has been written or recorded about his family and early life. His parents may have immigrated to the United States from Australia; his father is believed to have been an Australian Aborigine (original native people of the Australian continent). Granville Woods had a brother and a sister. His formal education ended when he was ten years old.

MACHINES AND ELECTRICITY

After leaving school, Woods began working as an apprentice in a machine shop. Along with acquiring the knowledge and skills of a machinist, he learned the trade of a black-smith.

1888: Creates overhead electrical conducting system for railways.

1890: Invents an electric incubator for hatching eggs.

1896: Creates a device for dimming theater lights.

1910: Died in New York City, on January 30.

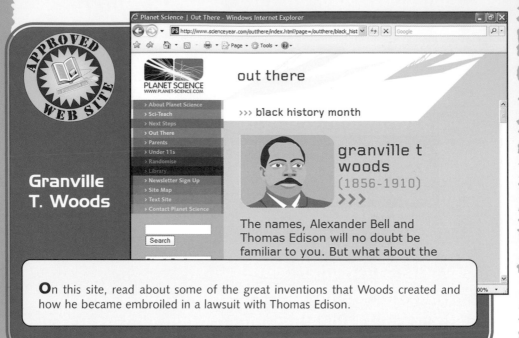

On this site, read about some of the great inventions that Woods created and how he became embroiled in a lawsuit with Thomas Edison.

Access this Web site from http://www.myreportlinks.com

In 1872, Woods moved to Missouri where he worked as both a fireman and an engineer for the Danville and Southern Railroad. While working there, Woods became fascinated with reading and learning all about electricity. At that time, African Americans were routinely denied borrowing privileges at public libraries. Woods got around that by having friends check out books for him.

When he was twenty, Woods moved east in search of a better job and educational opportunities. During the day, he worked at a machine shop in New York City. At night, Woods studied mechanical engineering at a local college. That led to his being hired as an engineer on a British steamer, the *Ironsides*.

Working on the steamer allowed him to travel and learn about steam engines and thermal power. Within two years, he was promoted to chief engineer on the *Ironsides*.

After two more years at sea, Woods was ready to settle down. He moved to Cincinnati, Ohio, and opened a factory that manufactured telephone, telegraph, and electrical equipment.

PATENTS AND "TELEGRAPHONY"

In 1884, Woods received the first of his many patents for an improved steam-boiler furnace. His furnace provided a more efficient method of combustion. The same year, Woods got a patent for a telephone transmitter. Woods's transmitter improved the sound quality of telephones by using alternating, instead of direct, current. The very useful device was able to transmit the human voice over longer distances with a louder and more distinct sound.

Woods's third patent in 1885 was for a device that combined the telegraph with the telephone for sending and receiving messages. Woods coined the word "telegraphony" to describe the process. Before Woods's invention only a telegrapher skilled in using the Morse code could send or receive a message by telegraph. A telegraph is a

GRANVILLE T. WOODS.

**The Electrician and Mechanical Engineer,
Cincinnati, O.**

The above is the picture of Granville
T. Woods, America's first colored electrician and mechanical engineer. He
was born in Columbus, Ohio, some
thirty-odd years ago. When quite a
boy he was put to work in a machine
shop. After learning the machinist's
trade he left for the West and became
a locomotive engineer. While not on
duty he experimented with and studied

▲ Many of Woods's inventions modernized transportation and
communication. He invented a device called a "telegraphony"
combining the telegraph with the telephone for sending and receiving
messages.

device that uses coded signals sent electronically over wires for communicating. Woods's machine allowed a user to switch quickly and conveniently between a telegraph and a telephone.

Thanks to Woods's invention, telephone calls could now be made at telegraph stations. Telegrams and telephone calls could now be transmitted over the same line without using different devices. Woods sold the invention to the American Bell Telephone Company for an undisclosed sum.

🧪 LINKING COMMUNICATION

In 1887, Woods patented one of his most important inventions. He called it the "Synchronous Multiplex Railway Telegraph." It became more commonly known as the induction telegraph system. This important invention allowed for messages to be sent between moving trains and from moving trains to railroad stations.

Prior to Woods's invention there was not any way for trains and railroad stations to contact one another. The lack of communication made rail travel dangerous. An engineer could not be warned about hazardous conditions like a stalled train on the track or a washed-out bridge. The engineer would not know until he saw the obstacle. By that time, it could be too late to safely stop the train.

Woods's invention, the "Synchronous Multiplex Railway Telegraph" made it possible for trains and train stations to contact one another. This helped engineers avoid accidents, making rail travel much safer.

Woods had noticed that telegraph lines often ran parallel to the railroad tracks. Woods's invention harnessed the power of static electricity to send messages through the telegraph lines. His method did not interfere with the regular use of the lines for sending messages. Because of Woods, train travel became much safer.

Woods's success with the induction telegraph system led to lawsuits by other companies and inventors. The Phelps Company was working on a similar device and they sued to challenge Woods's patent. So did Thomas Edison in two court cases.

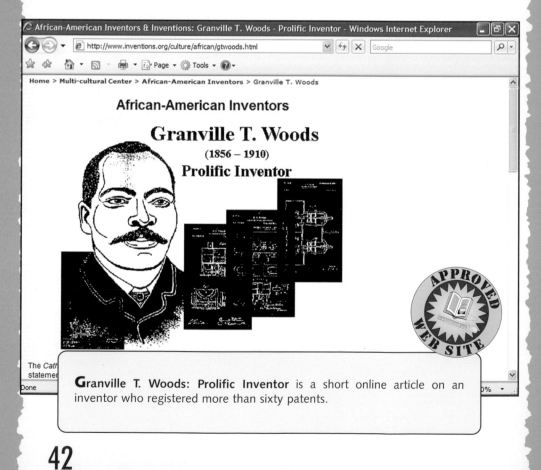

African-American Inventors & Inventions: Granville T. Woods - Prolific Inventor - Windows Internet Explorer

http://www.inventions.org/culture/african/gtwoods.html

Google

Home > Multi-cultural Center > African-American Inventors > Granville T. Woods

African-American Inventors

Granville T. Woods
(1856 – 1910)
Prolific Inventor

Granville T. Woods: Prolific Inventor is a short online article on an inventor who registered more than sixty patents.

Woods won every time, but the suits were costly and time consuming. At one time, Edison offered Woods the opportunity to become a business partner. Woods declined because he preferred to work alone.

When he was not preoccupied with legal matters, Woods continued to be a prolific inventor. Estimates vary on exactly how many patents he received. They range from thirty-five to more than sixty.

🧪 SAFETY FIRST AND OTHER CONCERNS

Many of Woods's inventions helped to modernize transportation. His electrical inventions made it possible to go from costly and inefficient steam-driven trains to more economical and efficient electrical models. In 1888, Woods created an overhead electrical conducting system for electric railways.

Woods's system used a pole that connected the train or trolley car to overhead electrical lines, which powered the locomotive's electrical engine. Woods is also credited with inventing the third-rail system now used by many urban subways. In all, Woods was granted fifteen patents in the field of electrical railways.

From 1902 to 1905, Woods invented a series of devices that improved the performance of the automatic air brake in railroad cars. That further

HALL OF FAME
overview
search
induction info
invention channels

PROGRAMS
overview
camp invention
collegiate inventors
contests
club invention
inspiring invention
independent inventors

WORKSHOP
overview
how to patent
resources

ABOUT INVENT NOW
overview
donate
sponsors
contact us
museum
USPTO museum
board
press

invent now
National Inventors Hall of Fame®
Foundation, Inc.

Invent Now

Fostering the inventive spirit in all of us.

Invent Now has put together an index of inventors, along with a brief biography for each. You can also search by invention to find the name of the inventor. A step-by-step guide to patents is also available.

EDITOR'S CHOICE

Access this Web site from http://www.myreportlinks.com

increased the safety of rail travel. Those inventions were bought out by the Westinghouse Air Brake Company.

Outside of transportation, Woods had other significant inventions. In 1890, Woods invented an electrically powered incubator for hatching chicken eggs. The use of an electrically controlled thermostat allowed the incubator to maintain a constant temperature. The thermostat Woods used was similar to the ones presently used in home heating systems.

Woods never liked electricity being wasted. In 1896, he invented a circuit-breaker type of apparatus that set up a separate current for powering and dimming theater lights. Before then, one resistor was used to control the current that powered other electrical devices in a theater. The resistor would get very hot and would become a fire hazard. Electrical energy would be lost in the form of heat. Woods's useful invention made theaters safer and also led to a 40 percent reduction in the theater's electric bills.

Unfortunately, Woods was victimized by the economic and business practices of his time, as well as for the color of his skin. When he marketed his products to larger companies, he received small profits. When he sold his patents to large companies, such as Edison's General Electric Company, the Westinghouse Electric Company, and the American Bell Telephone Company, he received no royalties.

When he died on January 30, 1910, Woods had little money. Legal fees from lawsuits had kept him from the prosperity that he so richly deserved.

George Washington Carver

As the son of slaves, George Washington Carver knew what it was like to be poor. He could have made a lot of money by patenting his agriculture-based inventions, but sharing and imparting knowledge were more important to him than making money. Carver only patented three of his estimated

Lifeline

1890: Accepted to Simpson College.

1894: Becomes first African American to graduate from Iowa State.

1864: Born in Diamond, Missouri, on July 12.

1891: Transfers to what is now Iowa State University.

five hundred inventions. "God gave them to me," Carver once explained. "How can I sell them to someone else?"[1]

CHILDHOOD

Carver was born on July 12, 1864, in Diamond, Missouri. Carver's father, who was a slave on a nearby farm, was killed in an accident shortly after George was born. It is not known whether Carver ever knew his father. Sometime in 1865, Carver was permanently separated from his mother and sister. There are conflicting accounts on how it happened.

One account is that they were kidnapped and taken to Arkansas. Another account claims that their owner, Moses Carver, sent them there to avoid being kidnapped. Carver's mother and sister were never seen or heard from again. George was returned to Carver's farm by one of Moses's neighbors.

Chapter 4

1896: Earns Masters of Science degree in agriculture.

1941: George Washington Carver Museum opens at Tuskegee Institute.

1939: Receives Roosevelt Medal for distinguished service to Science.

1943: Dies in Tuskegee, Alabama, on January 5.

When Carver was returned, he was gravely ill with whooping cough, a bacterial disease that causes uncontrollable coughing. He remained frail and sickly all through his childhood. Instead of doing hard physical labor, Carver did tasks such as laundry, sewing, and cooking. During his free time, Carver developed his keen interest in plant and animal life. He collected flowers and tended a small garden.

Moses's wife, Mary, soon noticed George's great desire and ability to learn. She gave him a spelling book and a Bible. George learned how to

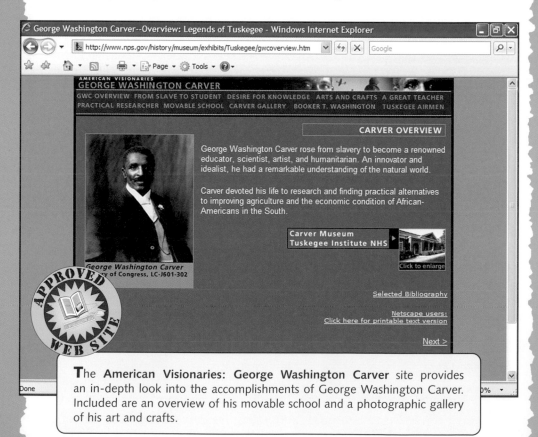

The **American Visionaries: George Washington Carver** site provides an in-depth look into the accomplishments of George Washington Carver. Included are an overview of his movable school and a photographic gallery of his art and crafts.

spell, read, and memorize passages from the Bible. He wanted to go to school, but African Americans were not allowed to attend the public school in Diamond, Missouri. Even though the Civil War was over and slavery was abolished, many states—especially those in the South—implemented segregationist laws denying African Americans rights and opportunities.

George Washington Carver was determined to get an education. He learned that there was a school for African-American children in Neosho, Missouri, which was eight miles from his home. The Carvers gave George permission to leave home to attend school. There are differing accounts of how old George was then. Some say that he was about fourteen, while other sources claim that he was only ten.

Carver did not stay at the school at Neosho for very long. He quickly realized that the teacher did not know much more than he did. During his teens, Carver roamed through Kansas, Minnesota, Iowa, and Colorado. He supported himself by doing odd jobs and going to school when he could. Eventually, he graduated from a high school in Minneapolis, Kansas.

DETERMINATION CONTINUES

In 1885, Carver applied, and was accepted at a small college in Highland, Kansas. When he arrived on campus, though, the school president turned him away because of his race. In 1890, Carver found a college that would accept him— Simpson College in Indianola, Iowa. After one year there, he transferred to Iowa State Agricultural College (now called Iowa State University) in Ames.

At Iowa State, Carver studied agriculture and botany. In 1894, he became the school's first African-American graduate when he earned a bachelor of science degree in agriculture. Then he became the first African American to serve on the school's faculty. In 1896, he earned a master's degree in agriculture.

Along with his teaching at Iowa State, Carver was in charge of the college's greenhouse. He used the greenhouse as a lab for conducting experiments in plant propagation (reproduction) and cross-fertilization. Carver's work began to be cited in scientific papers. He also traveled throughout Iowa giving lectures on botany and mycology (the study of fungi). Carver soon established a reputation as a respected teacher, scholar, and scientist.

Carver's work attracted the attention of the famous African-American educator and leader Booker T. Washington. Washington was the founder and president of the Tuskegee Institute, an African-American college in Alabama. Washington asked Carver to leave Iowa State to create

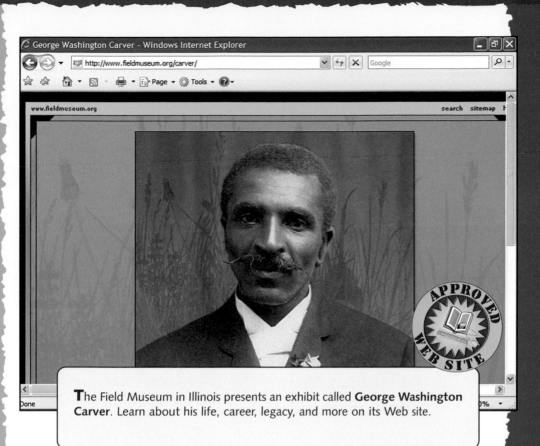

The Field Museum in Illinois presents an exhibit called **George Washington Carver**. Learn about his life, career, legacy, and more on its Web site.

and manage an agriculture department at Tuskegee.

Washington recruited Carver by writing: "I cannot offer you money, position, or fame. The first two you have; the last, from the place you now occupy, you will no doubt achieve. These things I now ask you to give up. I offer you in their place work—hard, hard work—the task of bringing a people from degradation, poverty, and waste to full manhood."[2]

Carver was very excited by the challenge that Tuskegee presented. He quickly accepted

Washington's offer. When Carver arrived at Tuskegee, he found that the only facilities for the agriculture department were a barn, a cow, a few chickens, and a twenty-acre patch of mostly barren land. He got a small group of students to scavenge for materials that could be used as lab equipment. They gathered pots, pans, wires, and tubes and made the tools and devices needed for experiments.

🧪 CROP ROTATION

One of Carver's early accomplishments at Tuskegee was getting local farmers to practice crop rotation. Many of the local farmers planted only cotton, year after year.

Eventually, the cotton crop would remove nutrients from the topsoil. Carver did soil tests and discovered that a lack of nitrogen in the soil was causing poor harvests.

Carver already knew that certain plants in the pea family, such as the peanut, take nitrogen from the air and deposit it into the soil. He began advising farmers to alternate cotton planting with planting peanuts. This helped to replenish the soil with nitrogen and restore high cotton yields. Then he started an outreach program and traveled to rural areas of Alabama to teach crop rotation and other modern farming methods.

▲ George Washington Carver said that learning skills like farming was "the key to unlock the golden door of freedom" for African Americans.

Named after the legendary inventor and scientist, the Carver Museum is located on the campus of the Tuskegee Institute in Tuskegee, Alabama.

As a result of Carver's outreach program, there was a dramatic increase in peanut crop production. But because so many bushels of peanuts were flooding the market, the price of peanuts plummeted. Carver now had a new challenge— finding increased uses for the peanut to increase its market value. That led Carver to invent and discover about 325 different products that could be made from peanuts.

Some of the peanut products Carver created include face powder, printer's ink, shampoo, dyes, and wood stains. Farmers were finding that peanuts were a more profitable crop than cotton or tobacco. Carver's success with the peanut led him to find multiple uses for other food crops like the sweet potato and the pecan.

Carver is credited with discovering 118 products that could be made from the sweet potato. Some of the better known sweet potato products are ink, dyes, starch, flour, and synthetic rubber. During World War I, the U.S. Army used Carver's sweet potato for making a cheaper loaf of bread, because there was a shortage of wheat for making flour.

An Altruist

As Carver's fame grew, some famous men tried to lure him away from Tuskegee. One unconfirmed story says that Thomas Edison offered Carver a

Learn more about the men and women inventors who shaped the fabric of American innovation at **Famous Black Inventors: A Rich Heritage Gives Way to Modern Ingenuity**.

EDITOR'S CHOICE

yearly salary of more than one hundred thousand dollars to join his staff at his world famous lab in Menlo Park, New Jersey. Famed auto tycoon Henry Ford supposedly also made Carver a generous job offer that Carver turned down. He even received an offer from the new government in Russia. The Russians were recruiting scientists and skilled workers by the hundreds to help build the new Soviet Union.[3]

Money and material possessions were never important to Carver. He often forgot to deposit his

paychecks. As many as six paychecks would pile up before Carver would cash or deposit them. Improving the lives of others was much more important to him. Carver expressed that goal by saying, "It has always been the one great ideal of my life to be of the greatest good to the greatest number of people."[4]

Carver died on the Tuskegee campus on January 5, 1943. He left his life savings of thirty-three thousand dollars to establish the George Washington Carver Foundation. Today, the foundation provides scholarships to Tuskegee students who hope to carry on Carver's work.

George Washington Carver (bottom row, center) with his staff at Tuskegee around 1902.

Madam C. J. Walker

Madam C. J. Walker's faith and determination in pursuing her dreams made her a wealthy and very successful businesswoman. Beginning with only $1.50, Walker developed a line of hair care products for African Americans. Those products would make Walker the first African-American woman in the United States to become a self-made millionaire.

Lifeline

1878: Walker's family leaves Louisiana.

1900–1905: Perfects hair-care formula for women.

1867: Born Sarah Breedlove in Delta, Louisiana, December 23.

1885: Walker's daughter, A'Lelia, is born.

Walker's full name was Sarah Breedlove McWilliams Walker. She was born in Delta, Louisiana, on December 23, 1867. Her parents, Minerva Anderson and Owen Breedlove, worked as sharecroppers.

Walker endured extreme poverty as a child. She lived in a windowless shack with a dirt floor and no water or toilet. The shack had no beds, so Walker, her parents, and an older brother and sister all slept on the dirt floor.

As sharecroppers, Walker's parents rented the land they farmed and lived on. They tried to earn a living by planting and picking cotton. When they harvested their cotton crop, they had to give one half to two thirds of it to the landlord. They sold what was left and attempted to live off of those funds.

1906: Embarks on auto tour to sell her products.

1919: Died in Irvington, New York, on May 25.

1905: Moves to Denver, Colorado.

1910: Employs 5,000 saleswomen.

Madam C. J. Walker was born in Delta, Louisiana. Her parents were sharecroppers who lived in poverty, much like the couple shown here.

Walker's parents died when she was seven. For the next few years, Walker and her sister, Louvenia, worked to keep the family's one-room shack. During the week they toiled in the cotton fields. On weekends, they worked washing other people's clothes. But in 1878, the price of cotton fell so low that they had to leave Louisiana.

Their brother, Alex, had moved to Vicksburg, Mississippi, so they followed him there. They found work as washerwomen. Louvenia married a man named Jesse Powell. Powell was a cruel man who was abusive to his wife and Walker. Walker escaped his abuse by marrying a man named Moses McWilliams when she was fourteen.

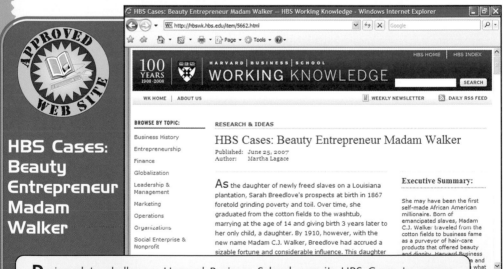

HBS Cases: Beauty Entrepreneur Madam Walker

Designed to challenge, Harvard Business School uses its HBS Cases to expose students to real world business situations. Learn some of the techniques that Walker employed to become a successful entrepreneur.

Access this Web site from http://www.myreportlinks.com

Walker's life with McWilliams was happier, but it was not any easier. She continued working as a washerwoman and McWilliams took whatever odd jobs he could find. In 1885, A'Lelia, their only child, was born. Two years after that, McWilliams was killed. It may have been an accidental death, but the details are unknown. One account claims that McWilliams died when an angry mob hung him.

In a Dream, A Wonderful Invention

At the age of nineteen, Walker became a widow and a single parent. Hoping for a better life, she and Lelia moved to St. Louis, Missouri. The best job she could find was working fourteen-hour days, washing, starching, and ironing clothes.

Although she was barely out of her teens, Walker soon began to lose her hair. The causes were years of poverty and poor diet along with working around chemical fumes while doing laundry. Yet another factor was the method that many African Americans used at that time for straightening their hair.

The method was known as wrap and twist. The hair would be divided into sections and a string would be tightly wrapped around each section. Then the section would be twisted. The method made the hair less curly, but constant use led to hair loss and scalp problems.

65

Walker began treating her own hair loss with patent medicines. She also began working on her own formula for stopping hair loss. Sometime between 1900 and 1905, Walker perfected her hair care formula for African-American women. She said that the formula came to her in a dream after she prayed to God for a way to save her hair:

> He answered my prayer, for one night I had a dream, and in that dream, a big black man appeared to me and told me what to mix up for my hair. Some of the remedy was grown in Africa, but I sent for it, mixed it, put it on my scalp, and in a

Visitors to the official **Madam C. J. Walker** Web site will find a number of interesting features, including a time line, photographs, biographies, and links to a number of audio and video files related to this African-American inventor.

few weeks my hair was coming in faster than it had ever fallen out. I tried it on my friends; it helped them. I made up my mind to begin to sell it.[1]

Walker called the first product she developed Wonderful Hair Grower. It was developed to stop hair loss and encourage the growth of new hair. Her second product was Glossine. It was sold as a light oil that both straightened hair and gave it a more radiant sheen. A third product, Vegetable Shampoo, cleaned the scalp and hair by removing dandruff.

It is generally believed that sulfur was the secret ingredient that Walker used in her highly successful hair care products. When combined with other ingredients, sulfur would soften and moisturize hair as well as work at curing dandruff.

Walker is also credited with popularizing an improved version of the hot comb. The original hot comb was a French invention. Walker's hot comb had wide gaps between the teeth for use on curly, thick hair. Walker's comb would be heated over a stove or an open flame and then used with Glossine to straighten hair.

SELF-MADE SUCCESS STORY

In 1905, Walker moved to Denver, Colorado, to live with a sister-in-law and her four nieces. Six months after moving there, she married Charles Joseph (C. J.) Walker. She began calling herself

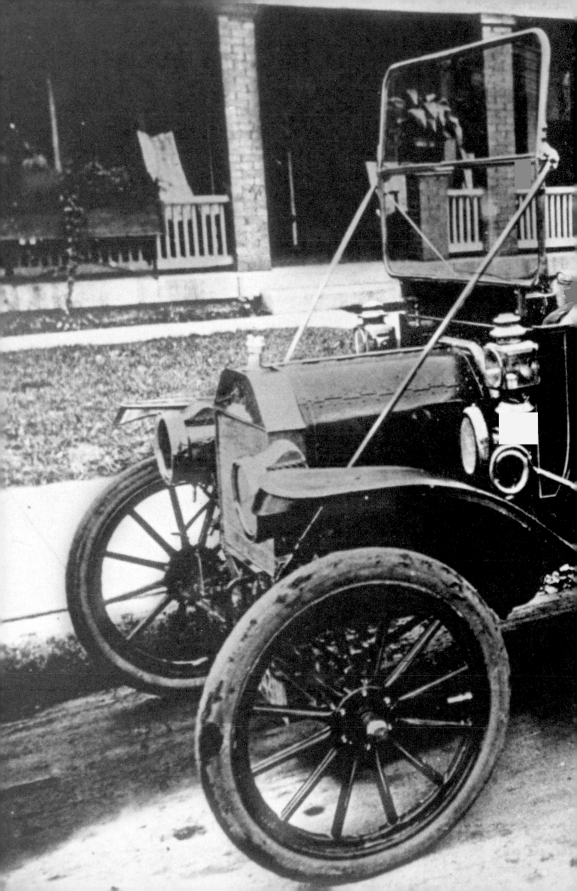

Madam C. J. Walker was a self-made millionaire who hoped to inspire other African Americans through her hard work. In this photo, Walker is wearing a dark coat and a hat that has a large feather.

Madam C. J. Walker and named her business The Madam C. J. Walker Manufacturing Company.

C. J. Walker had worked as a sales agent for a St. Louis newspaper and had some practical experience in promoting and advertising products. Through the use of flyers, posters, and newspaper ads, he helped his wife market and promote her products. Madame Walker built up sales by going door-to-door in Denver neighborhoods and giving free demonstrations of her products. Thanks to aggressive marketing and a willingness to take risks, Walker's company grew and prospered.

In the fall of 1906, she embarked on an extended auto tour to promote and peddle her products. She traveled extensively in southern and eastern states giving demonstrations and lectures at African-American clubs, schools, churches, and homes. Walker also used the tour for recruiting other African-American women to sell and promote her products.

By 1910, Walker had more than five thousand African-American women selling her products. She further expanded her business by establishing a chain of beauty parlors in the United States, South America, and the Caribbean. Walker's success allowed her to build her own factories and laboratories that utilized the most modern equipment available.

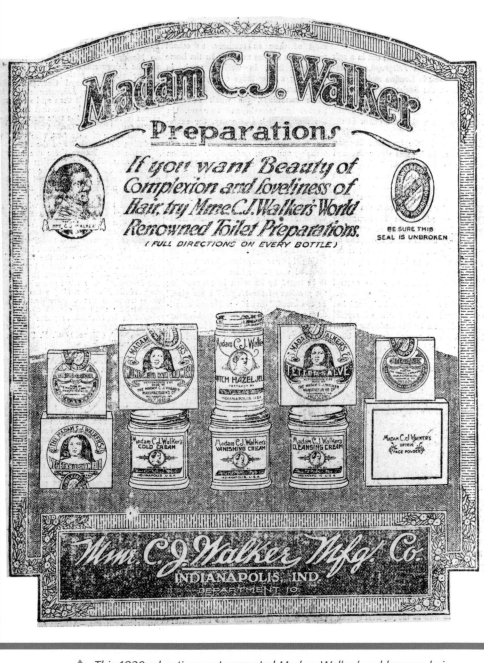

▲ *This 1920 advertisement promoted Madam Walker's cold cream, hair, and complexion products. At this point in time Walker had died, yet her company remained successful.*

Along with door-to-door and mail-order sales, Walker's agents taught other African-American women how to set up beauty parlors in their homes and the basics of bookkeeping. At its peak, Walker's company was employing more than twenty-five thousand women as sales agents and bringing an estimated half a million to 1 million dollars a year in sales.

Many African Americans disapproved of Walker's products. They accused her of attempting to make African-American women look more pleasing to whites by straightening their hair. Some African-American ministers denounced her products by saying that if God intended for African Americans to have straight hair; they would have been born with it.

WILL AND WORK

Still, Walker remains a model of a self-made African-American businesswoman who prospered though hard work and who also created jobs for thousands of African-American women. When she died on May 25, 1919, her estimated fortune was around 1 million dollars. By today's standards, she would have been a multimillionaire.

Walker used a good part of her fortune to support causes that fought racism and promoted civil rights. She also donated money to schools and colleges for African Americans.

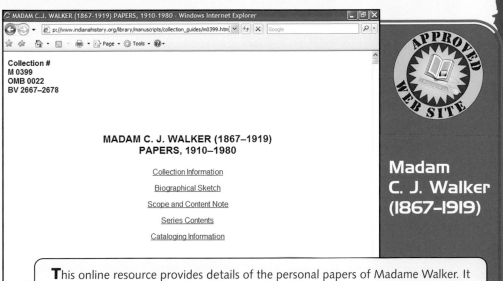

Access this Web site from http://www.myreportlinks.com

Walker firmly believed that success does not come easily and there was no substitute for hard work. She summed that up by saying: "There is no royal flower-strewn road to success. And if there is, I have not found it, for if I have accomplished anything in life it is because I have been willing to work hard."[2]

Garrett A. Morgan

Some people see problems and complain about them. Other people see problems and think about possible solutions. Garrett A. Morgan was an inventor who used his inventive mind to spot problems and create solutions for them. Morgan was born on a farm in Paris, Kentucky, on March 4, 1877. He was the seventh of eleven children. His mother, Elizabeth or Eliza Reed, was a former slave who had earned her freedom during the Civil War. His father, Sydney Morgan, was a railroad worker.

Lifeline

1901: Patents first invention, a belt fastener for sewing machines.

1914: Patents his "safety hood."

1877: Born in Paris, Kentucky, on March 4.

1907: Opens sewing machine sales and repair shop.

Morgan had little formal education. He completed elementary school before leaving home when he was fourteen. He settled in Cincinnati, Ohio, and found work as a handyman. Morgan knew that his lack of education was a handicap to finding a better job. He used part of his small salary to hire a tutor. Between handyman jobs, Morgan worked at improving his grammar and finding a job that paid more money.

Chapter 6

⚗ WHO SAYS TEN CENTS WILL NOT GET YOU ANYWHERE

After six years of working as a handyman, Morgan decided to look for a better job in Cleveland. In June 1895, he left Cincinnati with only ten cents in his pocket. Once in Cleveland he taught himself how to use a sewing machine

1916: Aids in rescue of construction workers.

1963: Died in Cleveland, Ohio, on August 27.

1914: Establishes National Safety Device Company.

1923: Patented first three-signal traffic light.

and found work as a sewing machine mechanic. Morgan had always been fascinated with mechanical devices. By 1901, he had already patented his first invention, a belt fastener for sewing machines.

Since he was ambitious and hardworking, Morgan decided to start his own business. In 1907, he opened his own sewing machine sales and repair shop. Business flourished and he was soon able to buy a house for his wife and children. He constantly thought of ways to improve the quality and versatility of his company's sewing machines. He added an attachment that made a zigzag stitch. Morgan also expanded his business by adding a tailor shop and a clothes-manufacturing plant. Eventually, Morgan's thriving business was employing thirty-two workers.

While working at his business, Morgan made an unexpected discovery that led to a unique new product. Most sewing machine needles operated at a high rate of speed. When sewing wool fabrics, the high speed of the needle caused the woolen material to get scorched. Morgan began experimenting with lubricating chemical solutions that would reduce the friction between the needle and the fabric.

One day, Morgan noticed that a solution he was working on caused the hairs on a pony-fur cloth to straighten. At first, Morgan tested the

Learn about the inventor at this **Garrett Morgan** Web page. Information on his invention of the gas mask and the first three-way traffic signal is included.

solution on a neighbor's Airedale terrier. Then he tried it on himself. Both times, the solution straightened the hair. Morgan began selling the solution as a hair-straightening cream. The product was a success and made Garrett Morgan a wealthy man.

THE SAFETY HOOD

Morgan's hair-straightening cream was a success, but it would not compare to his most important invention, the "safety hood," which he developed in 1912. The device served as a model for the modern-day gas mask. It was essentially a hood with an inlet for inhaling fresh air and an outlet for exhaling air. In his patent application, Morgan wrote that his invention would allow a "fireman to enter a house filled with thick suffocating gases and smoke and to breathe freely for some time."[1] The safety hood used a wet sponge to filter out smoke and toxic particles in the air.

Morgan's safety hood was patented in 1914 and won several awards. At the Second International Exposition of Safety and Sanitation, the invention won the First Grand Prize.

Morgan established the National Safety Device Company to sell, market, and manufacture the

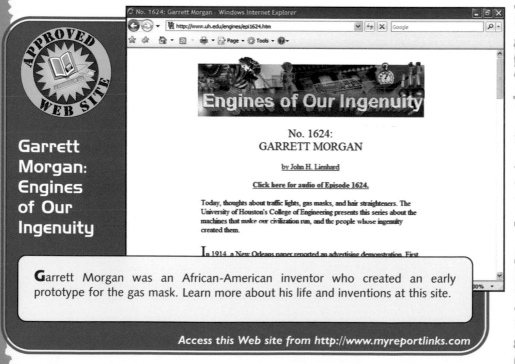

Garrett Morgan: Engines of Our Ingenuity

Garrett Morgan was an African-American inventor who created an early prototype for the gas mask. Learn more about his life and inventions at this site.

Access this Web site from http://www.myreportlinks.com

hood. Soon, fire and police departments all throughout America were ordering and using his invention. Orders also came in from chemists, engineers, and other workers who needed protection from harmful gases and fumes while they worked.

Even more orders poured in after Morgan and his brother, Frank, used the hood to rescue some trapped workers. In July 1916 an explosion in a tunnel being constructed 250 feet below Lake Erie trapped some workers. Rescue crews quickly arrived, but after entering the tunnel, they, too, succumbed to the smoke. Someone thought of Morgan and his invention, and so Morgan was summoned to the scene of the disaster.

Morgan and his brother Frank, along with two other volunteers, put on their safety hoods and bravely entered the dark, smoky, gas-filled tunnel. They carried the unconscious workers on their backs and brought them to safety. After repeated trips, they were able to save thirty-two workers. The city of Cleveland honored Morgan by awarding him a Medal of Bravery.

The daring rescue made nationwide news, but orders for the safety hood dwindled when people learned that Morgan was an African American. In fact, when Morgan demonstrated his invention in America's southern states, he had a white man demonstrate how his invention worked. During

Garrett Morgan (wearing a fireman's hat on the left, below) traveled the country in an effort to sell his "safety hood."

the demonstrations, Morgan pretended to be a Canadian Indian assistant named Big Chief Mason.

During World War I, the American forces made widespread use of Morgan's invention. During the war, chlorine and other gases were widely used to poison American soldiers. By that time, Morgan's invention was commonly known as the gas mask. Morgan had modified and improved his original invention. The new, improved gas mask carried its own air supply.

Along with a rifle and ammunition, Morgan's gas mask was standard equipment issued to American combat soldiers in World War I. The use of his gas mask is credited with saving the lives of thousands of soldiers.

MORGAN'S TRAFFIC SIGNAL

Morgan's next major invention is also credited with saving thousands of lives—the three-way traffic signal. Morgan got the idea for that invention after he saw a horse-drawn carriage collide with a car at an intersection in Cleveland. Even though police directed traffic and signals flashed stop and go, there were still frequent accidents and collisions. The stop-and-go signals were often ignored by motorists.

Morgan's invention used a tall pole with stop-and-go flaps that were raised and lowered by a

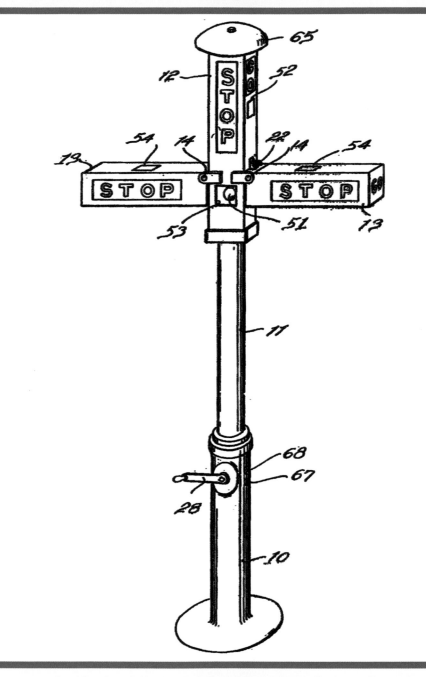

▲ *Morgan's three-way traffic signal is credited with saving thousands of lives. It was the model for today's red-yellow-green traffic lights.*

Who Made America? | Innovators | Garrett Augustus Morgan - Windows Internet Explorer

http://www.pbs.org/wgbh/theymadeamerica/whomade/morgan_lo.html

Google

Who Made America?   Innovators   Geography   Timeline   They Made America

DEMOCRATIZERS   GAMBLERS   REVOLUTIONARIES   PIONEERS

PREVIOUS INNOVATOR   NEXT INNOVATOR

Garrett Augustus Morgan
Affordable Gas Masks

The African American inventor of a life-saving device, mechanical traffic signals, and more had to fight for recognition.

Son of Freed Slaves
Garrett Morgan's safety hood saved the lives of countless firefighters and others. He was born in Kentucky during the Reconstruction era, in 1877. His father was the mixed-race son of a slave and a Confederate colonel, John Hunt Morgan. His mother, half Indian and half black, was the daughter of a Baptist minister. His race would impact Morgan's career profoundly.

Inventive Nature
Though Morgan only had a sixth-grade educa[tion] mechanical genius and an entrepreneurial be[nt] work in a textile factory, he learned how the worked, and became the only Negro adjuster improving mechanical problems. In 1907 he o[pened] repair shop, and soon launched a clothing busin[ess] wife, an immigrant seamstress from Bavaria. It w[as]

BORN: 1877, Paris, KY
DIED: 1963, Cleveland, OH

DID YOU KNOW?
Unable to sell his gas mask to fire departments in the South, Morgan hired an actor friend to

Garrett Morgan is known for inventing the traffic light and the safety hood. On the **Who Made America? Garrett Augustus Morgan** Web site from PBS, you can read about his inventions and view a photo of his safety hood.

Done

---

crank at the base. The device introduced a position between stop and go that was a forerunner to the yellow caution light seen on today's stoplights. Morgan patented the invention in 1923, but his experiences with sales of his gas masks caused him to sell the rights.

Morgan had seen how racism adversely affected the sales of his gas mask. He was no longer going to dress up like an American Indian and pretend to be someone else. He sold the rights to his traffic signal to General Electric for forty thousand dollars.

IMPROVING LIVES

When he was not working, Morgan concerned himself with trying to improve the lives of other African Americans. He founded a newspaper for African Americans called the *Cleveland Call*. He also dabbled in politics by running (unsuccessfully) for the Cleveland city council in 1931. His platform called for fair housing laws, relief for the unemployed, improved police protection, and better access to hospitals and health care.

Morgan's early experiments testing the gas mask eventually hurt his health. In 1943, he was diagnosed with the eye disease glaucoma. By 1950, he was nearly blind. Still, he continued to invent and experiment after he lost his sight. One of his last inventions was a pellet that would put out a cigarette if the smoker fell asleep.

Morgan died on July 27, 1963. Along with the legacy of his lifesaving inventions, Morgan's name lives on today. In 1997 the U.S. Department of Transportation began the Garrett A. Morgan Technology and Transportation Futures Program to encourage students to pursue careers in transportation and engineering.

Percy Lavon Julian

Although he dedicated his life to helping people see and ease their pain, Percy Julian could not avoid the blindness of bigotry and the pain of prejudice. In spite of that, he went on to improve the quality of life for millions of people suffering from glaucoma and arthritis.

Julian was born in Montgomery, Alabama, on April 11, 1899. He was the oldest of six children born to James and Elizabeth Julian. His father worked as a railway mail clerk. His mother was a teacher. Both James

Lifeline

1899: Born in Montgomery, Alabama, on April 11.

1920: Receives BS in Chemistry from DePauw University.

1923: Receives MS in Chemistry from Harvard University.

1931: Receives PhD in Chemistry from the University of Vienna.

and Elizabeth were deter-
mined that all of their
children would get a good
education. All six of the
Julian children would
earn college degrees.

🧪 SCHOOLING

Julian first showed an interest in studying chemistry
when he was a teenager,
but he was denied the opportunity to take
any classes. He had to attend a racially segregated high school that did not offer any
chemistry classes. Still, Julian excelled in the
classes he was allowed to take. In 1916, he
graduated at the top of his high-school class
and was admitted to DePauw University in
Greencastle, Indiana.

The segregated high school that Julian
attended had not prepared him for college.
During his first two years at DePauw, Julian
had to take remedial classes while working
his way through school. He worked as a waiter

Chapter

7

1953: Founded
Julian Laboratories.

1990: Elected to
National Inventors
Hall of Fame.

1994: U.S. Postal
Service issues stamp
in his honor.

1942: Develops
synthetic cortisone.

1975: Died in
Waukegan, Illinois,
on April 19.

NOVA | Forgotten Genius | PBS - Windows Internet Explorer

http://www.pbs.org/wgbh/nova/julian/

Google

Page ▾ Tools ▾

PBS HOME   PROGRAMS A-Z   TV SCHEDULES   SUPPORT PBS   SHOP PBS   SEARCH PBS

NOVA

Airing soon:
Dimming the Sun

HOME   TV SCHEDULE   SUPPORT   SHOP   WATCH ONLINE   TEACHERS   PODCASTS   RSS   SEARC

forgotten
GENIUS

Against all odds, African-American
chemist Percy Julian became one of
the great scientists of the 20th century.

APPROVED
WEB SITE

JULIAN THE   JULIAN SPEAKS

Percy Julian is the focus of this multimedia exhibition called **Forgotten Genius**. It includes photographs, a slide show, audio files, and a time line.

in a fraternity house and slept in the house's attic. Even with his heavy class schedule and workload, Julian graduated first in his class. In 1920, he received a bachelor of science degree in chemistry.

Julian decided that he would go on to graduate school and earn an advanced degree in chemistry. His father tried to talk him into studying medicine instead. James told his son that there would not be many jobs or career opportunities for African-American chemists. To his dismay, Julian discovered that his father was right.

A DePauw professor named William Blanchard tried to get Julian a fellowship to pay for his advanced studies in chemistry. Blanchard was unsuccessful and he told Julian what he had been told: "I'd advise you to discourage your bright colored lad. We couldn't get him a job when he's done, and it'll only mean frustration. . . . Why don't you find him a teaching job in a Negro college in the South? He doesn't need a PhD for that!"[1]

Julian was very disappointed, but he decided to try teaching for a while. He took a job teaching chemistry at Fisk University in Nashville, Tennessee. After two years at Fisk, he received a fellowship to study chemistry at Harvard University. In 1923, he earned his master's degree in chemistry from Harvard.

INTRODUCTION TO SYNTHESIS

But even with an advanced degree from a highly respected university, Julian had trouble finding suitable employment. He returned to teaching before earning another fellowship. The General Education Board and a wealthy friend from Harvard gave Julian the funds to study in Vienna, Austria.

The fellowship allowed Julian to study under Ernst Spath, an Austrian chemist who was famous for finding ways of synthesizing chemicals. Spath taught Julian about organic chemistry. Julian became interested in finding new uses for the soybean. His major interest was in using living cells to create materials that could cure illnesses in human beings.

In 1931, Julian received his doctorate in organic chemistry from the University of Vienna. He returned to the United States and resumed teaching. He taught at Howard, then at DePauw. While at DePauw, Julian made one of his famous discoveries.

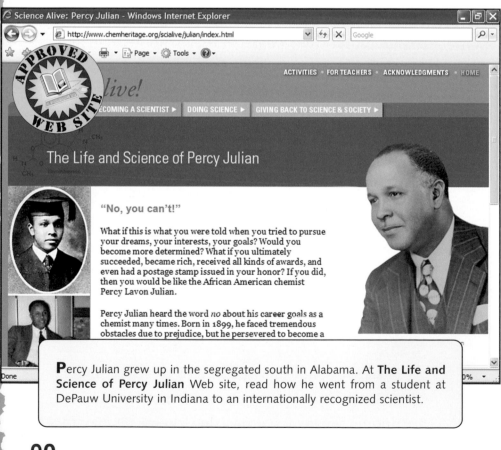

Percy Julian grew up in the segregated south in Alabama. At **The Life and Science of Percy Julian** Web site, read how he went from a student at DePauw University in Indiana to an internationally recognized scientist.

Julian had been studying the way in which natural substances in soybeans could produce a drug called physostigmine that was used to treat the eye disease glaucoma. In the early 1930s, an African plant, the Calabar bean, was the only source of physostiginc. If the drug could be made synthetically, there would be a much larger and less expensive supply for treating glaucoma. Thousands of people would then benefit from the less expensive drug.

🧪 LIKE PEAS IN A POD

After three years of intensive research and study, Julian and his assistants thought that they had found a way to make a synthetic form of physostigmine. But before they could be sure of it, the synthetic version would have to pass one final test.

Different substances have different melting points where they turn from the solid to the liquid form. If the natural and the synthetic form had the same melting point, then they were identical. During the tests, the two compounds melted at the same moment and at the same temperature. They were identical.

For nearly a century, scientists had tried in vain to synthesize physostigmine. Besides treating glaucoma, the drug had also been used as a treatment for swelling of the brain, leukemia,

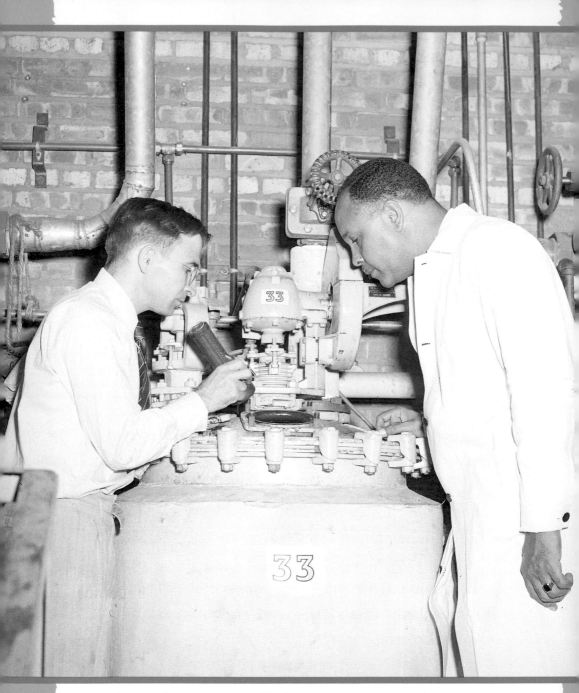

▲ Dr. Julian (right) is joined by his former student, Dr. Arthur Magnani, as they watch the progress of the manufacture of a drug in July 1947. Over his career, Dr. Julian was granted more than one hundred patents for his inventions and discoveries.

bronchial asthma, and skin and kidney disease. When Julian's discovery was reported in the *Journal of the American Chemical Society*, many chemists and scientists sent him their congratulations.

In spite of his great success, Julian still encountered racial discrimination. DePauw denied him a promotion to become the head of their chemistry department. The University of Minnesota declined to hire Julian because of his race. He decided to leave college teaching.

Julian then became the director of research and chief chemist for the Glidden Company in Chicago, Illinois. He became the first African American to direct a major industrial laboratory.

🧪 WORK WITH SOYBEANS

While working at Glidden, Julian was able to continue his research on the uses of the soybean. Julian's first project at Glidden was to find a way to make casein from soybeans. Casein was used to make paints more waterproof and to coat papers so that the ink on them would not smear. At that time, casein was made from milk.

Julian could not synthesize an exact match, but he found how to extract a soybean protein that was very similar to casein. His discovery was less costly than casein and was successfully used in paper coating, textiles, and paints. In just one year, Julian's discovery made Glidden's soybean

▲ Working with soybeans, Dr. Julian found a way to create a waterproof texture used in paints, paper, and textiles. He also used soybeans to create foam used to fight fires. These soybeans are ripe for picking.

division a profit of $135,000. The year before that, the same division had a loss of $35,000.

Another important soybean product was Julian's invention of a firefighting foam. A soybean extract and a stream of water produced a foam that would smother fires fueled by oil or gasoline. The product was widely used during World War II. It was officially called Aero-Foam, but it was nicknamed "bean-soup" by the sailors who used it. Similar fire-smothering products are still in use today.

Julian's work with soybeans also led to the manufacture of synthetic hormones used to treat cancer and to help prevent miscarriages. Prior to Julian's discoveries, the hormones were made from the brains and spinal cords of cattle. It was a slow and expensive process. Julian's synthetic hormones greatly increased the supply of the medicine and reduced the expense of hormonal treatments.

The synthesizing of cortisone from soybeans may have been Julian's greatest achievement. It occurred in 1949 while he was working for Glidden. Cortisone had been widely used for the relief of arthritis pain, but it had many other uses. It had also been used to treat allergies and asthma. As an ointment, cortisone is used to relieve itching caused by poison ivy, poison oak, and insect bites.

95

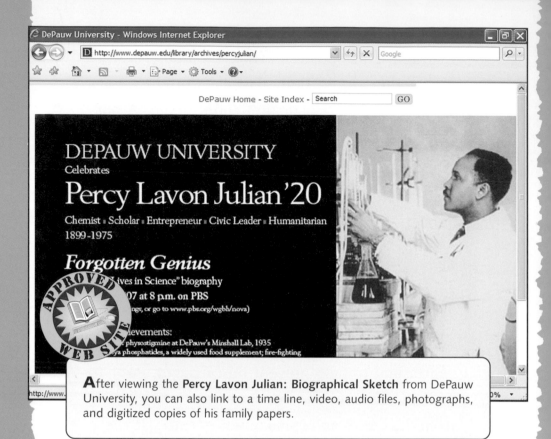

DePauw University - Windows Internet Explorer

http://www.depauw.edu/library/archives/percyjulian/

Google

DePauw Home - Site Index - Search   GO

DEPAUW UNIVERSITY
Celebrates
Percy Lavon Julian '20
Chemist ▪ Scholar ▪ Entrepreneur ▪ Civic Leader ▪ Humanitarian
1899-1975

Forgotten Genius
ives in Science" biography
07 at 8 p.m. on PBS
ngs, or go to www.pbs.org/wgbh/nova)

ievements:
physostigmine at DePauw's Minshall Lab, 1935
ya phosphatides, a widely used food supplement; fire-fighting

http://www.

After viewing the **Percy Lavon Julian: Biographical Sketch** from DePauw University, you can also link to a time line, video, audio files, photographs, and digitized copies of his family papers.

Unfortunately, cortisone was extremely expensive to make. In its natural form, cortisone is found in the bile of oxen and other animals. It would take the bile of more than fourteen thousand oxen to produce enough cortisone to treat one patient for one year. When Julian's synthetic cortisone was introduced in 1951, it cost thirty-five dollars a gram. Before that, natural cortisone sold for several hundred dollars a gram.

In 1953, Julian left Glidden and founded his own company, Julian Laboratories. Six years later, he sold the company for over $2.3 million. Julian continued his work as long as his health permitted. When he died on April 19, 1975, he had been granted more than one hundred patents for his inventions and discoveries.

Some of Julian's greatest honors came after his death. In 1990, he was elected to the National Inventors Hall of Fame. Julian and George Washington Carver became the first African-American inventors to receive that honor. Four years later, the United States Postal Service honored Julian by issuing a stamp with his portrait.

Patricia Era Bath

Imagine never knowing what it is like to see your reflection in a mirror or what the color green looks like. Try pouring yourself a bowl of cereal with your eyes closed. The likelihood is that you will have a mess to clean up before you are able to

Lifeline

1942: Born in New York City on November 4.

1959: Selected for National Science Foundation summer program.

1964: Graduates Hunter College with a BS in Science and Physics.

1968: Receives her MD from Howard University.

take your first bite. Eyesight is something that people often take for granted. After it is lost or badly diminished, people become aware of what a precious gift it is. Patricia Bath has dedicated her life to helping improve and sometimes restore that gift.

Chapter 8

Bath was born in the Harlem section of New York City on November 4, 1942. As a child, Bath read about Dr. Albert Schweitzer and his work as a medical missionary in Africa. His work treating leprosy (a disease that causes swellings, loss of sensation, deformities, and muscle deterioration) inspired her to pursue a career in medicine. Yet, she credits her parents for being her greatest inspiration. "Mom and Dad were the fuel and engine of my empowerment," Bath said.[1]

Her father, Rupert, was both well educated and well traveled. He had worked as a merchant

1977: Cofounded American Institute for the Prevention of Blindness.

1993: Retires from UCLA.

1974: Joins faculty at UCLA.

1988: Awarded patent for Laserphaco Probe.

seaman, and he gave Patricia a lifelong urge to travel and see the world. Her mother, Gladys, gave Patricia a love of books and reading. She nurtured Patricia's interest in science by giving her a chemistry set. Gladys worked to ensure that Patricia and her younger brother would get the best education possible.

"My mother was a housewife who worked as a domestic after we entered middle school," Bath said. "She scrubbed floors so I could go to medical school."[2]

⚗ ENTERING OPHTHALMOLOGY

Bath began winning science awards and honors when she was in high school. In 1959, she was

Patricia Bath

Patricia Bath is an African-American ophthalmologist who invented a device that helps remove cataracts with a laser. Learn more about her invention on this site.

Access this Web site from http://www.myreportlinks.com

selected to attend a National Science Foundation summer program for high-school students. Bath did work on cancer research and developed a mathematical equation to predict the growth of cancer cells. Her work not only won Bath national recognition, it gave her a belief in the power of her ideas.

After completing high school in just two-and-a-half years, Bath went on to Hunter College in New York City to study chemistry and physics. She received a bachelor of science degree in those subjects in 1964. Straight from there, she attended medical school at Howard University in Washington, D.C. Bath fondly remembers Howard as her introduction to studying and working with African-American professors and scholars.

"It was electrifying and uplifting to be exposed to black people who represented academic excellence, and I had wonderful mentors, Dr. LaSalle, D. Leffall, Jr., and Dr. Lois A. Young."[3]

After graduating with honors from medical school, Bath began studying and interning in ophthalmology. She worked in eye clinics at Harlem Hospital (1968–69) and Columbia University (1969–70). That was when she noticed that blacks were much more likely than whites to be blind or visually impaired.

"It seemed that at the eye clinic at the Harlem Hospital, half the patients were blind or visually

impaired. In contrast, at the eye clinic at Columbia
. . . there were very few obviously blind patients.
. . . I reached the conclusion that the cause for the
high prevalence among blacks was due to the lack
of access to ophthalmic care."[4]

Bath worked to correct the problem by propos-
ing a new academic discipline. The discipline was
known as Community Ophthalmology. It combined different aspects of community medicine,
public health, and clinical ophthalmology to provide primary eye care for the poor. Trained
volunteers visit day care and senior centers and
screen people for glaucoma, cataracts, and other
conditions that cause visual impairment. Vision
tests are given and eyeglasses are handed out.

LASERPHACO

In 1974, Bath moved to the West Coast to join the
faculty of University of California—Los Angeles
(UCLA) as a professor of ophthalmology. She also
became an assistant professor of surgery at
Charles R. Drew University, located in the same
city.

While at UCLA in 1981, Bath got the idea of
using laser technology to remove cataracts.
Cataracts are cloudy spots that form in the lens of
an eye. They cause distorted or blurry vision and
sometimes blindness. They often occur in people
sixty or older and almost everyone who lives long

Lemelson Center Invention Features: Patricia Bath - Windows Internet Explorer

http://invention.smithsonian.org/centerpieces/ilives/bath/bath.html

Google

INNOVATIVElives

The Right To Sight: Patricia Bath

by Martha Davidson

Enabling the blind to see is the greatest joy of Dr. Patricia Bath, eye surgeon, professor of ophthalmology, inventor of the Laserphaco Probe for the treatment of cataracts, and founder of the American Institute for the Prevention of Blindness. An independent thinker, she has been a trailblazer for women and African Americans in the medical profession, being the first to attain many of the highest academic honors and appointments in her field.

In March 2000, Bath talked about her life and work with students from three schools as part of the Lemelson Center's Innovative Lives series. Students from Thoreau Middle School in Virginia and Evans Middle School in Washington, D.C., met with her at the National Museum of American History, while classes from the Martin Luther King Elementary School in Los Angeles participated through video conferen students to follow their own career interests, to give back to their comm in the power of their own ideas. "Believe in the power of truth," she tol your mind to be imprisoned by majority thinking. Remember that the limi the limits of imagination."

Patricia Bath, M.D., S—
photo by Jeff Ti—

African-American inventor, Patricia Bath, is a trailblazer in the medical profession. **The Right to Sight: Patricia Bath** Web article will help you find out about her work as an eye surgeon, professor, and inventor.

enough will eventually develop them. They are also one of the leading causes of blindness.

Bath believed that using a laser to remove cataracts would greatly streamline the surgical procedure. A laser is a device that produces an intense, highly concentrated beam of single wavelength light. By using a laser, the cataracts could be removed more quickly and accurately. A laser procedure would also be less invasive since a smaller cut would be used to remove the cataracts.

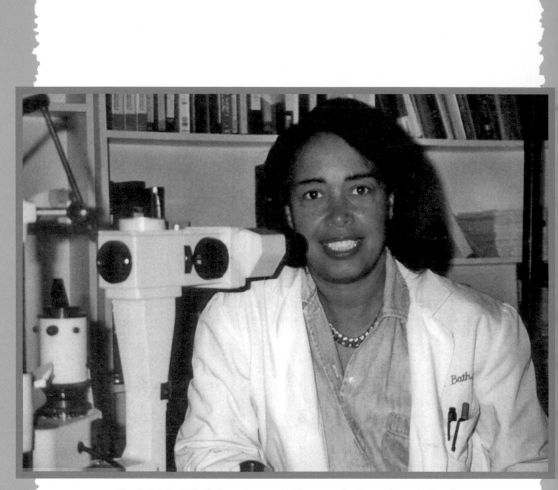

▲ Dr. Patricia E. Bath is a pioneer in the use of using a laser to treat eye disease. Her invention, called the Laserphaco, allows eye doctors to remove cloudy spots on the lens of the eye, called cataracts.

Unfortunately, Bath's idea was more advanced than the existing technology. It would take her nearly five years of testing and research before she could apply for a patent. "When I talked to people about it, they said it couldn't be done," Bath recalled.

"UCLA did not have the lasers I needed. We don't have a national laser institute. Our laser superiority is mostly weapon/military related."[5]

After designing her laser probe device, Bath traveled to Berlin, Germany, to test it. The most advanced laser equipment was available there. Her invention, which she called the Laserphaco, worked as she had hoped. After doing further testing at labs in California and New Mexico, Bath applied for a patent for Laserphaco.

In 1988, Bath received her first U.S. patent for the Laserphaco Probe. But when she tried to patent other applications of the Laserphaco, progress was very slow. Finally, Bath decided to proceed without using her patent attorneys. "I was getting nowhere," Bath explained. "Finally I decided to educate myself and I learned how to file a patent."[6]

RESTORING THE GIFT OF SIGHT

From 1998 to 2000, Bath was granted three additional patents relating to the Laserphaco. She has also patented her invention in Japan, Canada, and

African Americans .com

WELCOME TO
AFRICANAMERICANS.*com*

SEARCH

> go

Welcome to African Americans.com

Home

History

Heritage

Civil Rights

People

AfricanAmericans.com provides information on civil rights, history, current affairs, arts, and African-American heritage, along with biographical profiles of important people.

EDITOR'S CHOICE

Access this Web site from http://www.myreportlinks.com

five European countries. Profits from the sales and licensing of the Laserphaco have gone to support one of Bath's favorite projects—the American Institute for the Prevention of Blindness (AIPB).

Bath and three of her colleagues founded the AIPB in 1977 with the idea that eyesight is a basic human right. The AIPB believes that primary eye care should be available to people worldwide, regardless of their economic status. The institute has also promoted global initiatives to provide newborn infants with vaccinations and medications to prevent blindness and eye disease.

On a trip to North Africa, Bath experienced her personal best moment. It happened when she was able to restore the eyesight of a woman who had been blind for thirty years. "The ability to restore sight is the ultimate reward," Bath says.[7]

After retiring from UCLA in 1993, Bath has continued to do research on preventing blindness and developing new technologies for eye surgery. Bath continues to encourage young people to think outside of the box and not to put limits upon themselves.

"Believe in the power of truth. . . . Do not allow your mind to be imprisoned by majority thinking. Remember that the limits of science are not the limits of imagination."[8]

Lonnie G. Johnson

The jobs of "NASA scientist" and "squirt gun inventor" will not usually be found on the same person's résumé, but they can be found on Lonnie Johnson's. Along with working for NASA, Johnson invented the Super Soaker, which has become a best-selling toy. During the 1990s, more than 10 million Super Soakers were sold in the United States. Millions more have been sold in other countries.

Lifeline

1972: Receives BS in Engineering from Tuskegee University.

1949: Born in Mobile, Alabama, on October 6.

1975: Receives MS in Nuclear Engineering from Tuskegee University.

🧪 THE PROFESSOR

Johnson was born in Mobile, Alabama, on October 6, 1949. He was the third of six children. His father, David, was a civilian employee for the U.S. Air Force. His mother, Arline, worked as a nurse's aide.

Lonnie Johnson was always curious about how things worked. As a child, he took his toys apart to see how they were made. He also salvaged things like old jukeboxes and motors so he could tinker with them. Because of his inquisitive nature, Lonnie was nick-named The Professor.

In junior high school, Johnson kept pursuing his interests in science and rocketry. He found those activities more important than hanging out at the mall or watching television. Once, he caused an explosion in his mom's kitchen by mixing up some rocket fuel

1982: Dreams up idea for the Super Soaker.

1999: 250 millionth Super Soaker is sold.

1985: Founded what is now Johnson Research and Development.

2008: Develops JTEC system, which may greatly lower the cost of solar energy.

on her stove. He got the recipe from a library book. His parents were upset, but they tolerated his behavior. "[M]y father just made me take it outside," Johnson said. "They put up with what I did. They supported it."[1]

When he was a senior in high school, Johnson won an engineering contest by designing and building a four-and-a-half-foot robot. He built the robot from parts he gathered from a junkyard, a jukebox, family toys, and the neighborhood hardware store. He named the robot Linex and he operated it by using a remote control and compressed air. His accomplishment amazed his family and friends. "Back then, robots were unheard of, so I was one of the few kids in the

Engineer at Play: Lonnie Johnson; Rocket Science, Served Up Soggy

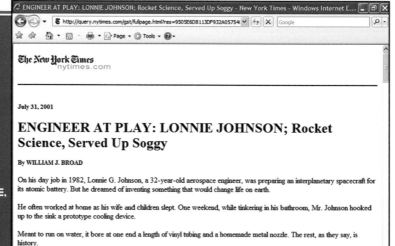

ENGINEER AT PLAY: LONNIE JOHNSON; Rocket Science, Served Up Soggy

By WILLIAM J. BROAD

On his day job in 1982, Lonnie G. Johnson, a 32-year-old aerospace engineer, was preparing an interplanetary spacecraft for its atomic battery. But he dreamed of inventing something that would change life on earth.

He often worked at home as his wife and children slept. One weekend, while tinkering in his bathroom, Mr. Johnson hooked up to the sink a prototype cooling device.

Meant to run on water, it bore at one end a length of vinyl tubing and a homemade metal nozzle. The rest, as they say, is history.

Invented by Lonnie Johnson, the Super Soaker is a powerful and popular water gun. This *New York Times* article explains how Johnson went from engineer to toy maker and how he turned it into a business.

Access this Web site from http://www.myreportlinks.com

country who had his own robot," Johnson recalled.[2]

After graduating from high school in 1968, Johnson attended Tuskegee University in Alabama on a math scholarship. In 1972, he graduated with a bachelor of science degree in mechanical engineering. Three years later, he earned his master of science degree from Tuskegee in nuclear engineering. Then he became an officer in the U.S. Air Force. He worked as a nuclear safety officer at the Air Force Weapons Laboratory in Albuquerque, New Mexico.

While working for the Air Force, Johnson discovered ways to improve the memory of computers used in space. He also devised a system for detecting enemy submarines. His important work earned him the Air Force Achievement Medal and the Air Force Commendation Medal. Johnson also won awards for his work with NASA on the Mars Observer and Galileo Jupiter Probe space projects.

THE BIRTH OF THE SUPER SOAKER

One day in 1982, Johnson was at home working on a new kind of heat pump that used water instead of Freon gas. While he was testing the cooling hose for his heat pump in the bathroom, a stream of water shot through the hose and blasted the shower curtain. "I thought, 'This would make

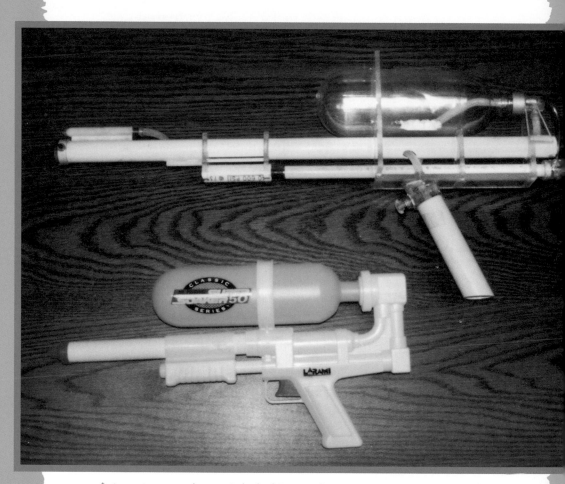

▲ Inventors spend a great deal of time and energy creating a prototype that works the way they want. The prototype of the Super Soaker is in the top of this photo, and one variety of the manufactured soaker is on the bottom.

a great water gun,'" Johnson said.[3] Thus, the Super Soaker was born.

Johnson designed the Super Soaker based on the principles of force and pressure. In other squirt guns, the force is limited to the strength of the shooter's trigger finger. With Johnson's invention, the shooter uses their entire arm to pump the gun. In turn, the gun stores energy. Each pump sends water from the gun's reservoir to an air chamber. When more water gets pumped in, the air gets compressed, or trapped.

When the trigger is pulled, the compressed air is released in a blast of water. "A small kid would not have enough strength to create the level of force needed to make the gun shoot a long way," Johnson explained. "So I had to put the energy in a little bit at a time."[4]

Johnson knew that he was on to making a great fun toy. Still, it took him around seven years to find a manufacturer for the Super Soaker. At different times, investors pledged to buy and market his squirt gun, but they would back out. Johnson had to stop inventing while trying to line up the financial backing for his toy.

Finally, Johnson got the break he needed. He took his Super Soaker to a big toy fair in New York City. He met a toy company executive named Al Davis who worked for the Larami Corporation.

▲ Johnson poses with a couple different models of The Super Soaker outside his office in Marietta, Georgia, on November 12, 1998.

"I turned around and there was the saddest guy that I'd ever seen," Davis said. "He'd been trying to find somebody who was interested in it (the Super Soaker). He told me that if we turned him down, he was going to give it up."[5]

Two weeks after meeting Davis, Johnson demonstrated the power of the Super Soaker to some Larami executives. He blasted some coffee cups off of the meeting room table. That was enough to convince them to buy Johnson's invention.

"I pumped it up and fired it across the conference room," Johnson recalled. "From that point it was a done deal."[6]

A Best Seller

The first Super Soakers hit the toy stores in 1990. The high-powered squirt gun became an immediate success. It became Larami's best-selling toy. By 1999, more than 250 million had been sold worldwide.

Unfortunately, sometimes kids misuse toys. In 1992, teens in New York and Boston were shot with real guns after engaging in Super Soaker fights. In some cities, mayors, police chiefs, and other officials said that the Super Soaker should be banned.

While Johnson cannot prevent a toy from being misused, he has taken steps to make it as safe as he can. A relief valve limits the pressure that can build up and be stored. The designers have also made the water stream fairly wide. That prevents the toy from any cutting action or from causing anything more painful than a mild sting. The toy also carries several warnings telling the user not to aim the squirt gun at anyone's face or eyes.

The huge profits from the Super Soaker have enabled Johnson to set up his own company, Johnson Research and Development. He continues to test and create new inventions. Currently, Johnson

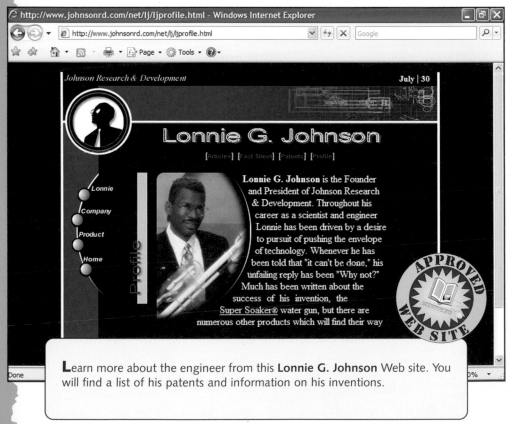

Learn more about the engineer from this **Lonnie G. Johnson** Web site. You will find a list of his patents and information on his inventions.

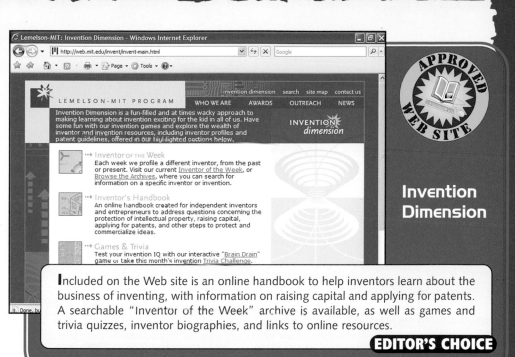

Access this Web site from http://www.myreportlinks.com

has been awarded more than eighty patents and he has more than twenty inventions awaiting patent approval. Some new inventions in the works include a home radon detector, new kinds of rechargeable batteries, and the Freon-free heat pump.

When *Inventor's Digest* magazine asked Johnson what advice he had for aspiring young inventors, he strongly emphasized that the most important thing was not giving up. "Perseverance!" Johnson exclaimed. "There is no short easy route to success."[7]

Report Links

The Internet sites described below can be accessed at
http://www.myreportlinks.com

▶**African American Inventors**
Editor's Choice This is an Edison International article on the achievements of African Americans.

▶**AfricanAmericans.com**
Editor's Choice This Web site celebrates African-American culture and history.

▶**Famous Black Inventors: A Rich Heritage Gives Way to Modern Ingenuity**
Editor's Choice Read short biographies of some famous African-American inventors.

▶**Invention Dimension**
Editor's Choice MIT offers this great resource for news on inventions and famous inventors.

▶**Invent Now**
Editor's Choice On this site, browse a database of inventors and learn how to patent an invention.

▶**United States Patent and Trademark Office**
Editor's Choice This government Web site offers step-by-step instructions on how to register a patent

▶**Against All Odds**
This *American Heritage* article discusses inventor Jan Matzeliger.

▶**American Visionaries: George Washington Carver**
The National Park Service offers a digital exhibit on Carver.

▶**Engineer at Play: Lonnie Johnson; Rocket Science, Served Up Soggy**
This *New York Times* article takes a look at the Super Soaker.

▶**Forgotten Genius**
This PBS site provides a look at the many accomplishments of Percy Julian.

▶**Garrett Morgan**
The Science Museum takes a look at prolific inventor, Garrett Morgan.

▶**Garrett Morgan: Engines of Our Ingenuity**
This is a biography and audio file for Garrett Morgan.

▶**George Washington Carver**
Learn more about George Washington Carver from this museum exhibit Web site.

▶**Granville T. Woods**
This Web site has an interesting biography of Granville Woods.

▶**Granville T. Woods: Prolific Inventor**
To find out more about Granville Woods, visit this Web site.

Report Links

The Internet sites described below can be accessed at http://www.myreportlinks.com

▶**HBS Cases: Beauty Entrepreneur Madam Walker**
Harvard Business School provides a look at cosmetics maverick Madam Walker.

▶**Inventor of the Week: Jan Matzeliger**
View this biography of inventor Jan Matzeliger.

▶**Lewis Howard Latimer**
General Electric's Web site provides good information on lighting and inventor Lewis Latimer.

▶**Lewis Howard Latimer: National Park Service**
This National Park Service article features Lewis Latimer.

▶**Lewis Latimer (1848–1928): Renaissance Man**
An article featuring the innovative life of Lewis Latimer.

▶**The Life and Science of Percy Julian**
This is an extensive overview of one of the country's pioneers.

▶**Lonnie G. Johnson**
Biographical information for Lonnie G. Johnson.

▶**Madam C. J. Walker**
This is the official Web site for inventor Madam Walker.

▶**Madam C. J. Walker (1867–1919)**
At this site, view the archival papers of Madam Walker.

▶**Matzeliger in 1924**
A biography and audio file for Jan Matzeliger.

▶**Patricia Bath**
Visit this MIT Web site for a short biography of Dr. Bath.

▶**Percy Lavon Julian: Biographical Sketch**
DePauw University presents an overview of Percy Julian's accomplishments on this site.

▶**The Right to Sight: Patricia Bath**
The Smithsonian Web site features the innovative life of Patricia Bath.

▶**Thomas Jennings**
Read a short biography of Thomas Jennings on this site.

▶**Who Made America? Garrett Augustus Morgan**
This Web site from PBS provides a brief overview of Garrett Morgan's life and inventions.

Any comments? Contact us: comments@myreportlinks.com

Glossary

abolitionist—A person who worked to end slavery.

arthritis—A medical condition in which joints become inflamed, causing pain.

bile—A yellowish liquid produced by the liver and used to break down fats.

botany—The study of plant life.

casein—An ingredient in paints and plastics.

cataracts—Cloudy spots on the lenses of eyes that impair vision and cause blindness.

circuit breaker—A device for stopping the flow of electricity through an electric circuit.

combustion—The act or process of burning.

cortisone—A liquid used to treat arthritis and other inflammations.

cross-fertilization—The union of two gametes (mature sex cells) from different individuals of the same species.

draftsman—Someone who draws plans and sketches for ideas such as machines and structures.

glaucoma—An eye disease that causes partial or complete loss of sight.

hormone—A substance formed by one organ of the body, which is sent to another organ.

laser—A concentrated beam of light.

millwright—A person who designs, builds, or repairs mills or mill machinery.

ophthalmology—The branch of medicine dealing with the treatment of the eye.

patent—A certificate that gives an inventor the right to improve upon and distribute his or her invention.

radon—A colorless radioactive gas.

resistor—A device designed to introduce resistance into an electric circuit to control the current.

royalties—Payments made to an inventor for each article sold under a patent.

schematic—A diagram of an electrical or mechanical system.

synthesis—The combining of separate elements or substances to form another element or substance. Making a new substance by mixing chemicals together.

synthetic—Something that is man-made, or artificial.

telegrapher—A person who sends and receives telegraph messages.

vaporize—The process of turning a solid or liquid into a gas.

versatility—Capable of several different uses or doing several different tasks.

Chapter Notes

Introduction

1. David Johnson, "Important Cities in Black History," *Fact Monster*, 2006, <http://www.factmonster.com/spot/bhmcities1.html> (January 25, 2007).

Chapter 1. Lewis Howard Latimer

1. Jessie Carney Smith, ed., *Notable Black American Men* (Detroit: Thomson Gale, 1998), p. 698.

2. USPTO Patent Full-Text and Image Database, "United States Patent: 0334078," *United States Patent and Trademark Office*, n.d., <http://patft.uspto.gov/netacgi/nph-Parser?Sect1=PTO1&Sect2=HITOFF&d=PALL&p=1&u=%2Fnetahtml%2FPTO%2Fsrchnum.htm&r=1&f=G&l=50&s1=0334,078.PN.&OS=PN/0334,078&RS=PN/0334,078> (June 18, 2007).

3. Dick Russell, *Black Genius and the American Experience* (New York: Carroll & Graf Publishers, Inc., 1998), p. 301.

Chapter 4. George Washington Carver

1. Kwame Appiah and Henry Louis Gates, Jr., eds., *Africana: The Encyclopedia of the African-American Experience* (New York: Basic Civitas Books, 1999), p. 389.

2. Columbus Salley, *The Black 100: A Ranking of the Most Influential African-Americans, Past and Present* (Richmond, Va.: Citadel Press, 1999), p. 108.

3. A. Blakely, as appears in Maxim Matusevich, ed., *Africa in Russia, Russia in Africa: Three Centuries of Encounters* (Trenton, N.J.: Africa World Press, Inc., 2007), chp. 1.

4. Susan Altman, *Extraordinary African-Americans* (New York: Children's Press, 2001), p. 97.

Chapter 5. Madam C. J. Walker

1. Jessie Carney Smith, ed., *Notable Black American Women* (Detroit: Gale Research Inc., 1992), p. 1185.

2. Madam C. J. Walker, as posted by Mary Bellis, "Famous Quotes from Madam Walker," *About.com: Inventors*, 2009, http://inventors.about.com/od/wstartinventors/a/MadamWalker_2.htm (April 28, 2009).

Chapter 6. Garrett A. Morgan

1. Otha Richard Sullivan, *African-American Inventors* (New York: John Wiley & Sons, Inc., 1998), p. 77.

Chapter 7. Percy Lavon Julian

1. Hamilton Bims, "Percy L. Julian's Fight for His Life," *Ebony*, March 1975, vol. 30, no. 5, p. 96.

Chapter 8. Patricia Era Bath

1. Martha Davidson, "The Right to Sight: Patricia Bath," *Smithsonian Museum*, n.d., <http://invention.smithsonian.org/centerpieces/ilives/bath/bath.html> (April 17, 2009).

2. Ibid., p. 2.

3. Ibid.

4. Ibid., p. 3.

5. Ibid., p. 5.

6. Ibid.

7. Changing the Face of Medicine, "Dr. Patricia E. Bath," *United States National Library of Medicine—National Institutes of Health*, n.d., <http://www.nlm.nih.gov/changingthefaceofmedicine/physicians/biography_26.html> (June 28, 2007).

8. "Dr. Patricia E. Bath," *Black History Pages*, n.d., <www.blackhistorypages.net/pages/pbath.php> (May 30, 2007).

Chapter 9. Lonnie G. Johnson

1. Fern Shen, "The Man Behind the Curtain (of Water)," *The Washington Post*, July 9, 2002.

2. Patricia J. Mays, "Rocket Scientist Blasts Off into Toyland . . . ," *Los Angeles Times*, February 7, 1999.

3. Ibid.

4. William J. Broad, "ENGINEER AT PLAY: LONNIE JOHNSON; Rocket Science, Served Up Soggy," *The New York Times*, July 31, 2001, <http://query.nytimes.com/gst/fullpage.html?sec=technology&res=9505E6D8113DF932A05754C0A9679C8B63&n=Top%2FNews%2FScience%2FTopics%2FInventions%20and%20Patents> (May 30, 2007).

5. Timothy Roche, "Soaking in Success," *Time*, December 4, 2000, <http://www.time.com/time/magazine/article/0,9171,998696,00.html> (May 30, 2007).

6. Mays.

7. Broad.

Further Reading

Altman, Susan. *Extraordinary African-Americans*. New York: Children's Press, 2001.

Hudson, Wade. *Book of Black Heroes: Scientists, Healers and Inventors*. East Orange, N.J.: Just Us Books, 2002.

Jones, Lynda. *Five Brilliant Scientists*. New York: Scholastic, 2000.

Kallen, Stuart. A *History of Free Blacks in America*. Detroit: Lucent Books, 2006.

Kramer, Barbara. *George Washington Carver: Scientist and Inventor*. Berkeley Heights, N.J.: Enslow Publishers, 2002.

McKissack, Fredrick, and Patricia McKissack. *Madam C. J. Walker: Self-Made Millionaire*. Berkeley Heights, N.J.: Enslow Publishers, Inc., 2001.

Moser, Kit, and Ray Spangenburg. *African Americans in Science, Math, and Invention*. New York: Facts On File, 2003.

Sims, Doris J. and Stephen Jackson. *The Breathing Mask: Garrett Morgan Inventor*. Los Angeles: Children's Cultu-Lit Book Co., 2005.

Sluby, Patricia Carter. *The Inventive Spirit of African Americans: Patented Ingenuity*. Westport, Conn.: Praeger, 2004.

Sullivan, Otha Richard. *African-American Women Scientists and Inventors*. New York: Wiley, 2002.

Index

A

Aborigine, 35
Aero-Foam, 95
Air Force Achievement
      Medal, 111
Air Force Commendation
      Medal, 111
Air Force Weapons
      Laboratory, 111
Albuquerque, New Mexico,
      111
American Bell Telephone
      Company, 39, 45
American Institute for the
      Prevention of Blindness
      (AIPB), 106
Ames, Iowa, 50
Anderson, Minerva, 61

B

Bath, Patricia Era, 98–107
Bath, Gladys, 100
Bath, Rupert, 99–100
Beal Brothers, 28
Bell, Alexander Graham, 10,
      14, 39, 45
Berlin, Germany, 105
Bible, 48–49
Blanchard, William, 89
Board of Patent Control, 19
Boston, Massachusetts, 11,
      13, 14, 115
Breedlove, Alex, 64
Breedlove, Louvenia, 64
Breedlove, Owen, 61
Brooklyn, New York, 17
Brown, Charles W., 13

C

Calabar bean, 91
Caldwell, Rev. Samuel, 11
Carver, George Washington,
      46–59, 97

Carver, Mary, 48
Carver, Moses, 47–48
Charles R. Drew University,
      102
Chelsea, Massachusetts, 11
Chicago, Illinois, 93
Cincinnati, Ohio, 37, 75
Civil War, 12, 49, 74
Cleveland, Ohio, 75, 79,
      82, 85
Cleveland Call, 85
Columbia University,
      101–102
Consolidated Lasting
      Machine Company, 33
Crosby, Halsted, & Gould,
      13

D

Danville and Southern
      Railroad, 36
Davis, Al, 113, 115
Delta, Louisiana, 61
Denlow, Charles H., 29
Denver, Colorado, 67, 70
DePauw University, 87–89,
      90, 93
Diamond, Missouri, 47, 49
Douglass, Frederick, 11
Dutch East Indies Company,
      24
Dutch Guiana (Suriname),
      23, 25

E

Edison, Thomas Alva, 10,
      14, 17, 19, 34, 42–43,
      45, 56
Edison Electric Light
      Company, 17

F

Fisk University, 89
Ford, Henry, 57

G

Garrett A. Morgan Technology and Transportation Futures Program, 85
Garrison, William Lloyd, 11
General Electric, 19, 45, 84
George Washington Carver Foundation, 59
Glidden Company, 93–96
Greencastle, Indiana, 87

H

Hammer & Schwartz, 20
Harlem, 99, 101
Harlem Hospital, 101
Harney Brothers, 25–26, 28
Harvard University, 89
Highland, Kansas, 49
Howard University, 101
Hunter College, 101

I

Incandescent Electric Lighting, 19
Indianola, Iowa, 50
Inventor's Digest, 117
Iowa State Agricultural College (Iowa State University), 50
Ironsides, 37

J

Jennings, Thomas L., 6
Johnson, Arline, 109
Johnson, David, 109
Johnson, Lonnie G., 108–117
Johnson Research and Development, 116
Journal of the American Chemical Society, 93
Julian, Elizabeth, 86

Julian, James, 86
Julian, Percy Lavon, 9, 86–97
Julian Laboratories, 96

L

Lake Erie, 79
Larami Corporation, 113, 115
LaSalle, Dr., 101
Laserphaco, 105
Latimer, George, 11–12
Latimer, Lewis Howard, 8, 10–21
Leffall, Jr., Dr., 101
London, England, 16
Lynn, Massachusetts, 25, 30

M

Madam C. J. Walker Manufacturing Company, 70
Matzeliger, Jan E., 21–33
Maxim, Hiram S., 14, 16–17
McWilliams, Moses, 64–65
Menlo Park (Edison), New Jersey, 57
Minneapolis, Kansas, 49
Mobile, Alabama, 109
Montgomery, Alabama, 86
Montreal, Quebec, 16
Morgan, Garrett A., 9, 74–85
Morgan, Sydney, 74

N

NASA, 108, 111
Nashville, Tennessee, 89
National Inventors Hall of Fame, 97
National Safety Device Company, 78–79
National Science Foundation, 101

Neosho, Missouri, 49
New York City, 14, 16, 20, 36, 99, 101, 113
Nichols, Melville S., 29
Norman, Winifred Latimer, 21

O
Oberlin University, 6
Olmstead Electric Lighting Company, 17

P
Pan-American Exposition (1901), 33
Paris, Kentucky, 74
Phelps Company, 42
Philadelphia, Pennsylvania, 16, 24
Powell, Jesse, 64

R
Reed, Elizabeth (Eliza), 74

S
Schweitzer, Dr. Albert, 99
Second International Exposition of Safety and Sanitation, 78
Simpson College, 50
Spath, Ernst, 89–90
St. Louis, Missouri, 65
Super Soaker, 108, 111, 113, 115–116

T
Tuskegee Institute (Tuskegee University), 50–52, 56, 59, 111

U
Union Lasting Machine Company, 29, 33
United States Electric Lighting Company, 14

United States Patent Act (1790), 5
United States Postal Service, 97
University of California— Los Angeles (UCLA), 102, 105, 107
University of Minnesota, 93
University of Vienna, 90
U.S. Air Force, 109, 111
U.S. Army, 56
U.S. Department of Transportation, 85
U.S. Navy, 12–13
U.S. Patent Office, 5, 30
USS *Massasoit*, 13

V
Vicksburg, Mississippi, 64
Vienna, Austria, 89–90

W
Walker, Charles Joseph, 69
Walker, Lelia (A'Lelia), 65
Walker, Madam C. J., 60–73
Washington, Booker T., 50–52
Washington, D.C., 101
Westinghouse Air Brake Company, 44
Westinghouse Electric Company, 19, 45
Woods, Granville T., 8, 34–45
World War I, 56, 82
World War II, 95

Y
Young, Dr. Lois A., 101